Richard Linklater |

Contemporary Film Directors

Edited by James Naremore

The Contemporary Film Directors series provides concise, well-written introductions to directors from around the world and from every level of the film industry. Its chief aims are to broaden our awareness of important artists, to give serious critical attention to their work, and to illustrate the variety and vitality of contemporary cinema. Contributors to the series include an array of internationally respected critics and academics. Each volume contains an incisive critical commentary, an informative interview with the director, and a detailed filmography.

A list of books in the series appears at the end of this book.

Richard Linklater

David T. Johnson

**UNIVERSITY
OF
ILLINOIS
PRESS**
URBANA,
CHICAGO,
AND
SPRINGFIELD

Frontispiece: Richard Linklater (*left*), with actor Jack Black (*center*) and
first assistant director George Sledge (*right*), on the set of *Bernie* (2012)

Library of Congress Cataloging-in-Publication Data
Johnson, David T., 1972–
Richard Linklater / David T. Johnson.
p.   cm. — (Contemporary film directors)
Includes bibliographical references and index.
Includes filmography.
ISBN 978-0-252-03692-7 (hardcover : alk. paper) —
ISBN 978-0-252-07850-7 (pbk. : alk. paper) —
ISBN 978-0-252-09404-0 (e-book)
1. Linklater, Richard, 1960–
—Criticism and interpretation. I. Title.
PN1998.3.L544J86   2012
791.4302'33092—dc23   2011034117

For Eileen

Contents |

Acknowledgments |

First, I want to thank James Naremore, whose initial encouragement and support throughout the project have been invaluable; at the University of Illinois Press, my thanks also goes to Joan Catapano, Daniel Nasset, Tad Ringo, Annette Wenda, Joe Peeples, and others whose hard work helped bring this book to fruition, and while not at the press itself (but as part of the process), I wish to thank Michael Koresky for taking the time to read and reflect on this manuscript. In Austin, I want to thank Richard Linklater, of course, both for the films themselves and for giving a long interview during a busy time of postproduction on *Bernie*, and my thanks also goes to Kirsten McMurray at Detour for always responding to every query, promptly and kindly. The Austin community lived up to its reputation as a generous one; not only did the Austin Film Society provide archival material, but Louis Black sent me a number of useful resources as well. Via email, author Joe Bonomo, whose terrific book on *Highway to Hell* guided my thinking on AC/DC, was kind enough to elaborate even further on the band. At Salisbury University, I want to thank Elsie Walker, James Burton, Adam Wood, and Jerry Miller, for being sounding boards on issues related to the project, great and small; I also thank Christine Smith, for last-minute help with the interview transcription, and Jack Wenke, who volunteered, unprompted, to read over the manuscript, and from which the book has undoubtedly benefited. More generally, I want to thank the Department of English, the Fulton School, the Blackwell Library, Instructional Design and Delivery, and my students, who continue to ask good questions and challenge me to think about cinema in new ways. At the University of Florida, my thanks goes to Robert Ray, a fabulous scholar and teacher whose ideas about cinema and the humanities continue to animate my thinking, and Gregory

Ulmer, for his thoughtful advice and good nature. And additionally my sincere gratitude goes to these scholars at other institutions, for their support: Christian Keathley, Thomas Leitch, and Brian Doan. Finally, I want to thank my friends, family, and especially Eileen for bearing with the writing process and encouraging me when I needed it most.

Richard Linklater |

Time Is a Lie |

Here are three moments from three different films, all directed by Richard Linklater:

1. In Paris, at the Shakespeare and Company bookstore, a group of journalists has gathered to hear a young writer discuss his book *This Time,* a semiautobiographical romance about a woman he met many years ago in Vienna. After deflecting a few questions on "what really happened," the writer describes his next project, a novel about a middle-aged man who, thinking about his life at present, suddenly finds himself pulled into the past, to a night in his adolescence. But this is not memory so much as two "nows," both experienced at once; as the writer explains, "it's obvious to him that time is a lie . . . it's all happening all the time, and inside every moment is another moment, all . . . happening simultaneously." Just then, a figure steps out from behind a bookcase: it is the woman from Vienna, nine years later.

2. In Colorado, a Mexican immigrant's husband has been injured on the job, and to make up for his lost earnings, she has returned to the slaughterhouse she had walked out of only months earlier, hoping never to return. To be rehired, she has submitted to degrading sexual encounters with the foreman, who now leads her, both dressed fully in white, through an industrialized killing floor, a Fordian nightmare of gears, levers, blood, and viscera that surround them while he shows her where she will be working. As she takes her position, her eyes, just above her white mask, well with first one tear and then another, the only evidence of emotion she permits herself on this, the first of many such shifts to come.

3. Somewhere in New England, at an apartment retrofitted for band practice, a group of junior high students plays a classic rock song—AC/DC's "It's a Long Way to the Top (If You Wanna Rock and Roll)." Unlike the world it describes, however, their immediate concern is less about paying one's dues and more about their solos, led by a manic lead singer—their former schoolteacher, who faked his way into the classroom and was subsequently fired, but not without igniting in them a passion for music. And now, in the after-hours space outside of the official school, the students play on, having a good time as they await the chorus and, very likely, finding themselves in sympathy with at least one of the lines their teacher sings—that creating such music, even in a friendly atmosphere so unlike that of the original song, is "harder than it looks."

Many readers have likely already recognized these films, all released within a three-year period: *Before Sunset* (2004), *Fast Food Nation* (2006), and *The School of Rock* (2003), respectively. On first examination, they are quite different projects: *Before Sunset* is an unlikely sequel to *Before Sunrise* (1995), both of them small-scale romantic melodramas; *Fast Food Nation* is as straightforward a critique of American industry (here, fast food) as has been put on screen in recent years; *The School of Rock* is a studio comedy that features Jack Black. Whereas other directors have moved from project to project without a clear pattern in mind, Linklater's work offers a particularly satisfying trajectory in this regard, with the choices in subject matter as surprising and interesting as the eventual films into which they are made. Consider that *The Newton Boys* (1998) followed *subUrbia* (1997), or *Tape* (2001) followed *Waking Life* (2001), or *Bad News Bears* (2005) followed *Before Sunset,* and it can become tempting to view the films as not having *any* discernible relation to one another other than the fact that they all share the same directorial credits in their title sequences.

Of course, this defiance of a basic pattern of authorship fits well with contemporary film studies, which tends to view director studies with skepticism, despite the enormous amount of work that continues to be produced in this area. One reason is simply the sense that any film is a collective venture, and certainly, Linklater has had his share of talented collaborators over the years, including writers, production designers, cinematographers (Lee Daniel has shot seven of his films), editors (Sandra Adair has edited all of them since *Dazed and Confused* [1993]), music supervisors, performers (Ethan Hawke has appeared in six of his films), producers (Anne Walker-McBay, John Sloss), and so many other above- and below-the-line workers who, quite simply, helped make these films happen. But skepticism toward director studies goes beyond acknowledging fruitful working relationships; it has a much longer, more complex critical history. Early director studies drew heavily on Romanticism, from which many of our associations about the individual artist spring, and this reliance on a format more suited for authors (or auteurs) distorted other subjects, including, in addition to the collaborative nature of a film's creation, the industrial contexts that affect production and reception, the historical moments in which films are made and seen, and the economic and social conditions, as well as the ideologies, that cinema both reveals and obscures. Yet director studies, perhaps more than any other area of film studies, have never gotten as far from its early days as it would have liked; this volume is unlikely to convince readers otherwise, given its chronological structure and interest in articulating some shared preoccupations among the films (ones that themselves draw on Romanticism). That said, many writers who reflect the more recent concerns I just outlined have informed my thinking, directly and indirectly, in the preparation of this text. (I should also say at the outset that I avoid more extensive production history because of another book published during the writing of this one, Alison Macor's

Chainsaws, Slackers, and Spy Kids: 30 Years of Filmmaking in Austin, Texas, an invaluable resource on Linklater's career and Austin film culture more generally.)

When it comes to longer critical studies about Linklater, however, sustained writing on the director has been infrequent. Thomas A. Christie's *Cinema of Richard Linklater,* the only existing book-length study, mostly restricts itself to basic narrative surveys and summaries of reception in the popular press, though a conclusion productively draws out some of the films' larger concerns, including "the search for the authentic," a "fascination with society and social mores," "the potentially dehumanising aspects of modern society," and the "theme of journeying" (184–95). Many essay-length pieces, though not as extensive as a book-length treatment would permit, have shed light on the filmmaker's work. Within academic film studies, both Lesley Speed and Mary Harrod have written ambitious career-study essays, and other scholarly treatments of individual films, also well worth the reader's time, have been penned by Robin Wood, Steven Shaviro, Markos Hadjioannou, Lynn Turner, Jon Radwan, Glen Norton, and others. In a book written for a more general audience, Derek Hill devotes a chapter to Linklater, seeing him as "the cautiously optimistic Truffaut from Austin" (40), and some excellent writing about Linklater has emerged online: Brian Price's profile on the *Senses of Cinema* "Great Directors" database, for example, provides an engaging reflection on his work, including a long-standing interest in "idleness," and the online film journal *Reverse Shot,* in the summer of 2004, held a "Linklater Symposium" that included many provocative short pieces on the films and one of the best longer interviews with Linklater to date. Also, now that so much print has been digitized, readers can access material previously available only to local publications, and the online archive of Linklater's hometown arts weekly, the *Austin Chronicle* (edited by Louis Black, who appears in a couple of Linklater's films), provides reviews and interviews going back several years. Still, despite the intelligence with which these examples and others have approached Linklater's work, longer studies have been virtually nonexistent. Might the unusual pattern among the films be the reason for this absence? Is it that Linklater himself has been ambivalent about cinema studies and the academy in the past? Or is it just that cinema studies quite often lags behind films with which it is contemporary, so that critical volumes tend to emerge only after a definable moment seems to have passed—a movement's dissipation, a director's falling out of or coming back into favor, or some other intuitive shift? Whatever the reasons for this absence, this study hopes to take part in a longer serious conversation about Linklater's films that recent writing suggests is only just beginning.

One important facet of that conversation, as it has emerged thus far, has been its investment in taking the aesthetic experience seriously, and in that respect, this book is no exception. Although one finds this same impulse in the writing surrounding almost any director, in Linklater's case, I suspect that part of the reason for this interest is that the films themselves so often encourage deep intellectual engagement with—and a healthy curiosity about—art, books, films, music, and other texts, from *anyone,* not just a professor in a particular academic discipline. (Lesley Speed has discussed this aspect of Linklater's films at length ["Possibilities"].) In this way, they resonate with humanities education more generally, at a time when university budgets are shrinking and humanities courses are often the first to go—because, after all, what do they *do*? One could ask the same of many of Linklater's protagonists, who are nonetheless deeply and thoughtfully engaged with their world and the issues they are most passionate about. This study is therefore partly about aesthetic pleasure and locates itself among much recent writing about cinema that does not regard such pleasure with suspicion—or at least as more complex than it has often been considered. I am thinking of cinephilia, that impulse that animates so much past and current writing about film, in the work of authors who appear in this volume and those who do not (and even those whose work I have yet to discover). Furthermore, the origins of my approach might be put even more directly: I like these movies, and I have enjoyed writing about them. Robin Wood, in his essay on *Before Sunrise,* describes wanting to "shar[e] my delight in it with others" (318), and my own impulse with these films is very similar. My hope is that this text will find readers accustomed to more specialized academic discourse and readers who are not—and that both will benefit from this extended investigation.

When considering what aspects these films have in common, certainly one of their most prominent features is a self-consciousness about their own influences. The films frequently make both direct and indirect references to a number of filmmakers associated with the arthouse cinema tradition, ones whose work has been screened over the years by the Austin Film Society, an organization that Linklater helped found in 1985 that is still very active in the Austin community. The influence of Robert Bresson, for example, is one Linklater has acknowledged, a connection not difficult to make to his second feature film, *Slacker* (1991) (Bresson's *L'argent* [1983] is often cited). Other international influences would include Andrei Tarkovsky, Carl Theodor Dreyer, Jean-Luc Godard, and Chantal Akerman, to name a few. And like many American directors of Linklater's generation, one sees the influence of New Hollywood in his work: George Roy Hill's *Butch Cassidy and the Sundance Kid* (1969) and *The Sting* (1973) hover over *The Newton Boys*; *Bad News Bears* is a remake of the 1976 film directed by Michael Ritchie; Monte Hellman's *Two-Lane Blacktop* (1971) and George Lucas's *American Graffiti* (1973) inflect *Dazed and Confused*; and Martin Scorsese's influence is also felt, whether in the specific allusion to *American Boy* (1978) in *Waking Life*, where Steven Prince retells a story from Scorsese's film, or *Dazed and Confused*, where the slow-motion sequence of Wooderson, Pink, and Mitch entering the Emporium to Bob Dylan's "Hurricane" recalls Johnny Boy's slow-motion entrance to the Rolling Stone's "Jumping Jack Flash" in *Mean Streets* (1973). Linklater also cites the importance of American avant-garde cinema in his work. Not only has he talked about the influence of James Benning on *It's Impossible to Learn to Plow by Reading Books* (1989), but he has also discussed Kenneth Anger's *Scorpio Rising* (1964) as the template for the opening of *The School of Rock*, a connection that arthouse cinephiles no doubt find humorous, given its preceding Dewey's failed stage dive. In this way, Linklater's richly allusive style takes pleasure in mixing, matching, and "remixing" the various cinematic influences that he and his collaborators have absorbed over the years.

Such allusions extend outward as well, into philosophy (*Slacker*, *Waking Life*), art (*Before Sunrise*), and especially literature. James Joyce, for example, is a figure frequently mentioned in relation to the films, given Linklater's repeated fascination with single-day narratives, much like *Ulysses* (a book read aloud from in *Slacker*). Also, as many commentators have pointed out, *Before Sunrise* takes place on June 16, or

Bloomsday, the day on which the narrative of *Ulysses* takes place. Beyond Joyce, the characters of Linklater's films are often well read. Consider the way books inform Jesse and Celine's romance, whether in the initial exchange at the outset of *Before Sunrise,* where she reads a collection of Georges Bataille's writing, as he reads Klaus Kinski's memoir *All I Need Is Love,* or in the location of *Before Sunset'*s initial reunion, Shakespeare and Company, which served as a hub of modernism (and which also originally published *Ulysses*). Jesse, himself a writer, also references Thomas Wolfe in the opening of that film—specifically, Wolfe's note to the reader, where he discusses the blurred line between fact and fiction for any writer. But Jesse and Celine are not the only characters for whom literature plays an important role. The protagonist of *It's Impossible to Learn to Plow by Reading Books* leaves the library with a copy of Cesare Pavese's *Burning Brand* tucked under his arm; Louis Mackey's professor character in *Slacker* is surrounded by books when he turns a potential home invasion into an opportunity for Socratic dialogue on the state of Austin and capitalism more generally; Mike consoles himself after the fight with Cliff in *Dazed and Confused* by comparing his escapades to Hemingway's (and the fact that, when biographers note that he was involved in a fight, they rarely cite the winner); *Waking Life* is loaded with literary references, among others; a budding writer's obsession with Keats's literary urn—and a real one—informs *Me and Orson Welles* (2009); and many of the other films present characters who read or indirectly make reference to other texts.

Linklater's films also share a more general kinship with other previous literary figures. In fact, when casting about for other influences, I found myself returning to an unlikely one: Henry David Thoreau (the casting metaphor here perhaps all too apt). Putting aside the obvious caveats in such a comparison—the different historical moments, the extreme contrasts between writing journal entries by a pond versus marshaling ten, twenty, one hundred people to create a single scene in a film—an interesting thread runs between them, a set of concerns that is central to this text's investigation of Linklater's films, which might be put as a fascination with temporality, particularly in attending to the present, even if such attendance is impossible to sustain, potentially naive, and, at times, even dangerous. Thoreau captures the possibilities a present temporality might offer in *Walden,* with the writer noting, "In any weather, at any hour of the day or night, I have been anxious to improve the nick of time, and notch it on my stick too; to stand on the meeting of two eternities, the past and future, which is precisely the present moment; to toe that line" (10). For Thoreau, of course, this meant a meeting with the divine: "God himself culminates in the present moment, and will never be more divine in the lapse of all the ages. And we are enabled to apprehend at all what is sublime and noble only by the perpetual instilling and drenching of the reality that surrounds us" (67). While Linklater's work is hardly religious in a traditional sense, it is very much interested in the experience of temporality, for both characters and spectator, and in particular in what it means to inhabit the present, whether beneficial or destructive, elusive or inevitable. In order to explore such ideas, time becomes less rigid in these films (Christie notes the "temporal pliability" of both *Before* films [127]), even as they make use of traditional narrative structures. One finds this expressed directly on occasion, as when Jesse confesses that "time is a lie" or when Linklater's character from *Waking Life* describes a dream encounter with Lady Gregory, Yeats's patron, who explains that time is really just "one instant":

> Actually, there's only one instant, and it's right now, and it's eternity. And it's an instant in which God is posing a question, and that question is basically, "Do you want to, you know, be one with eternity? Do you want to be in heaven?" And we're all saying, "No thank you—not just yet." And so time is actually just this constant saying "no" to God's invitation. I mean, that's what time is—I mean, and it's no more 50 A.D. than it's 2001, you know—I mean there's just this one instant, and that's what we're always in. And then she tells me that actually this is the narrative of everyone's life—that, you know, behind the phenomenal difference, there is but one story, and that's the story of moving from the "no" to the "yes." All of life is like, "No thank you, no thank you, no thank you." Then, ultimately, it's, "Yes, I give in. Yes, I accept. Yes, I embrace." I mean, that's the journey—I mean, everyone gets to the "yes" in the end, right?

Whether the viewer agrees with this admittedly extreme view of spiritual and physical time, one sees an investment in the present moment and the subjective experience of temporality, even if, here, the implication is that time itself is essentially a figment of our imaginations.

Such ruminations cannot help but resonate with recent writing in cinema studies itself, which has seen a resurgence of interest in film and time. André Bazin, the famous French film writer of the 1940s and 1950s who wrote that "the cinema is objectivity in time" (14), someone derided for years as hopelessly naive, has been, it can now be said, successfully recovered, the writing surrounding his work surpassing what even his most passionate advocates would have dreamed of two decades ago. Gilles Deleuze, a philosopher who wrote extensively on cinema and time (most notably in the *Cinema* volumes), has also enjoyed a renaissance of late, as has phenomenology more generally. And so many books and essays discussing "the end of cinema," beginning especially with the centennial of cinema in 1995, have even gone so far as to suggest cinema's time is now over, thereby making discussions of time itself all the more relevant. This body of scholarly interests thus serves as the context in which one might view this book, though my hope is that the approach here will provide a forum that readers both in and outside academic cinema studies will find accessible and stimulating. That approach might be summed up, generally, as the exploration of temporality, particularly one that celebrates an attendance to the present—one not divorced, it should be said, from the past or future—even as the films are as likely to explore this idea's darker implications and consequences.

For a celebration of being awake to the present, alert to the rich possibilities and "the perpetual instilling and drenching of the reality that surrounds us," in Thoreau's words, one need look no further than so many of the characters in the films who express that impulse in word and action, such as "Having a Breakthrough Day," a character in *Slacker* who is so struck by the experience, she can only reiterate that she is having just the kind of day she is named for; Wooderson, giving his fifty-yard-line "L-I-V-I-N" speech, in *Dazed;* Jesse and Celine, musing on time in the *Before* films; Willis, improvising his approach to bank robbery in *The Newton Boys;* Speed Levitch, presenting his ideas for an ongoing, living memorial in *Live from Shiva's Dance Floor* (2003); Jon, giving into the present moment in *Tape,* along with his acceptance of whatever consequences his past actions may bring; Dewey and Buttermaker, in their respective triumphs, both enjoying the present moment for its own sake, whether in the "one great rock show" of *The School of Rock* or the final losing game of *Bad News Bears;* and even Augie Garrido, whose coaching advice in *Inning by Inning* (2008) emphasizes a sense of being at play in baseball, despite the intense desire to win, as well as the entirety of *Me and Orson Welles,* where every day Richard spends with the famous character of the title seems to be a continually evolving awareness to what makes that moment unique, if not the evolving present tense of theater rehearsal and performance. Beyond that, Linklater's wandering narratives, in their playfulness and self-consciousness with screen time, also encourage an awareness of cinema's temporality as much as the experience of time that the characters inhabit. This is a fairly abstract notion, impossible to quantify from viewer to viewer, but it is nonetheless worth acknowledging as part of a larger body of interests. Consider *Slacker's* "Conspiracy A-Go-Go" author, whose monologue on the JFK assassination goes on at length, as the narrative, such as it is, all but comes to a halt; in these and other similar moments, we may find ourselves reflecting on cinematic time more generally and the ways that most narrative cinema avoids such slower pacing, despite the speed of the monologue's delivery. (I follow Jonathan Rosenbaum on this observation, who has written about a tendency in *The Newton Boys* to "stop the storytelling dead in its tracks.") Regardless, we see, in the present temporality of the bookstore in which this person speaks, just how passionate and interesting he is, even if we are encouraged to find the humor in the scene as well. Characters, in these films, are not afraid to debate and hold forth on their passions. Indeed, Linklater often depicts characters who seem almost naive at times in their interests—yet, in that naïveté, engaged, vibrant, and alive within an ongoing engagement with those passions and the present moment, one that the films' own periodic digressions encourage.

By the same token, a sense of the present is not without its darker implications. In Linklater's world, those implications are often tied to an ongoing critique of the idea of America. One thinks again of Thoreau, whether in the more famous passages describing the "lives of quiet desperation" of most people—a sense of "resignation," as he puts it, an "unconscious despair" that so many experience (4)—or many other meditations on the relentless demands of capitalism, as when he discusses the nation's factory system for clothes: "The condition of the operatives is becoming every day more like that of the English; and it cannot be wondered at, since, as far as I have heard or observed, the principal object is, not that mankind may be well and honestly clad, but, unquestionably, that the corporations may be enriched" (18). Such sentiments share an undeniable kinship with Linklater's films in a much darker present temporality, one where the past becomes malleable, even erased, and the present cultivates neither reflection nor intellectual engagement but, instead, relentless repetition, one that discourages creativity and stifles the democratic impulse. The most obvious examples would be *Fast Food Nation*'s characters, from slaughterhouse worker to corporate executive, who find no escape from the larger structures of industry and American consumption, a constant grinding away in the present that, in an obvious but effective metaphor, makes cattle of us all (if not cowards as well); the present-ness brought on by Substance D in *A Scanner Darkly* (2006), a drug produced by a corporation in conjunction with the American government, for the purpose of mollifying the masses and creating a target for the drug war; and the inhabitants of *subUrbia*'s Burnfield, who seem unable to leave the Corner, itself "timeless" in the worst possible way. Other examples appear elsewhere in the films. And while ultimately they seem optimistic and hopeful about the idea of the present, such darker aspects are never far from their ethos, which accounts for the fact that *The School of Rock* and *Fast Food Nation* were directed by the same person.

The following set of interests, then, guide this text: the attempt to attend to the present moment, despite the impossibility of sustaining such a disposition; the relationship of the present with the past and the future; the dangers of a present without a past or future, or a more dark version of the present moment; and the subjective, more "pliable" experience of temporality, in contrast to a more linear, scientific time. To be sure, many other pathways are possible. Films are dynamic objects that operate beyond the control of maker or audience, and recording one set of patterns among them is but one way to begin discussing them. My hope is that this study's focus will provide a basic sense of cohesiveness, while allowing for digressions that treat what is specific to each work, and encourage readers and writers to take up other conversations about the films, as they are rich and reward such attention. This text's conversations begin with the first full-length film in his body of work, *It's Impossible to Learn to Plow by Reading Books*, which was followed by the more well-known *Slacker*. To these two films, and the one that followed, *Dazed and Confused*, this study now turns.

Slowly Moving Trains, Welcome to Austin, and L-I-V-I-N

Texan by birth, a regional identity that weaves through several of his films, Richard Linklater grew up in the town of Huntsville and the city of Houston, where his mother and father lived, respectively. An aspiring fiction writer and, later, playwright, as well as a baseball player, Linklater attended Sam Houston State University for two years before leaving school. He would not return, instead living in Houston for a while, working for an oil rig based in the Gulf of Mexico, and then, eventually, making his way to Austin, Texas, where he first started making short films and where he continues to live (his production company, Detour Filmproduction, is located there as well). Along the way, Linklater has been a supporter of cinema in Austin in other capacities as well, notably through the Austin Film Society; some of his original collaborators there would be instrumental in the production of *Slacker* four years later. His persona is that of an affable creative figure who wears the artist's label lightly but no less seriously, and he is often characterized by a work ethic that goes back to his earliest days of making shorts and running the film society. These projects provided an education in cinema during his time in Austin in the mid-1980s, but the first three major films he directed would provide even more lessons: his first feature-length film, *It's Impossible to Learn to Plow by Reading Books*; his first national and international success, *Slacker*; and his first studio film, *Dazed and Confused*.

Shot on Super-8 and edited on video, *It's Impossible to Learn to Plow by Reading Books* begins with the main character in an apartment who listens to a cassette-tape "letter" from a college student complaining about his parents, a job, and studies, before inviting the listener to "blow off school" for a visit. The opening shot, positioned low to the ground so that we see only the protagonist's legs as he enters the front door, followed by a second long shot of the main room of the apartment, sets up the film's stylistic approach: long takes from static camera positions, ones that sometimes avoid more traditional framing and frequently observe events from a distance. The message also establishes one of the major motifs of the film—the human encounter with automated technology (radios, televisions, ATMs, vending machines) and as an extension of that, the recorded human voice (announcements at bus stations and train terminals, cassette tapes the protagonist listens to). After the opening, the film follows the character's mundane activities—walking to a mailbox, doing his laundry—before seeing him fire a gun from his window. But whereas such an incident might normally set up the plot, here, no chase gives way, nor are there any consequences. Instead, the film's ambiguity invites other readings: generic, in an ironic acknowledgment of what this film will not be, a thriller; historical, in a reference to Charles Whitman's shooting at the University of Texas in 1966, touched on again by Old Anarchist in *Slacker;* self-referential, as a pun on "shooting" a film; or many other associations. From here, the bulk of the film is a journey, as the protagonist travels by train to visit his friend in Missoula, Montana; to visit other West Coast locations (including San Francisco, also via train); and to return to Austin. Then, even after that return, the protagonist travels to a family reunion and his mother's house before returning, once again, to Austin. There is little in the way of a narrative climax; the film simply ends with the central character walking away from the camera as a street musician plays a song, in this case Keith McCormack, who appears again in *Slacker* playing "Disturbed Young Man with a Tan."

Much of the film, in fact, takes place while the protagonist is in transit. Of its eighty-five-minute length, approximately a third (roughly thirty-three minutes) is spent either in moving conveyances or in locations associated with them (bus stops, train stations, an airport, and so on). In addition to trains, the protagonist also travels by bus, car, streetcar, and even ferry. And as a kind of joke about its investment in travel, when the protagonist leaves his mother's house toward the end of the film, the car will not start, as the film cuts immediately to his sitting in a mechanic's waiting area. In this way, *It's Impossible* might loosely be considered a road movie, though one in which the "quest motif" that Timothy Corrigan (144) has noted as a feature of the genre is only ambiguously gestured toward and is likely not even existent. By the time we see the departure of the protagonist while the street musician plays, we are unlikely to be convinced that the protagonist has undergone any major shifts in his persona or gained anything fundamentally missing from his life at the outset. That said, the film's characterization of the road very loosely as a place of fascination, if not involving a "quest" per se, and its investment in trains in particular suggest that it draws on this tradition. Such interests are also evident in the name of Linklater's production company, Detour, named for the Edgar G. Ulmer road movie of 1945, and one could plausibly argue for reading much of Linklater's oeuvre as an extended riff on the genre, where the sort of wisdom Corrigan describes is quite often gained, in spite of what happens in *It's Impossible.*

Within the film's investigation of the road and journeying more generally, time often seems to slow; as the protagonist waits, we wait, unlike in other narratives that would waste little time moving to the more action-oriented scenes. In this sense, both stylistically and narratively, *It's Impossible* evokes structural filmmaking of the 1960s and 1970s avant-garde, a connection Linklater has made explicit ("Commentary—*It's Impossible*"). In *Visionary Film: The American Avant-Garde,* P. Adams Sitney famously defined the structural film as one that "insists on its shape, and what content it has is minimal and subsidiary to the outline" (407–8). If that definition seems a bit vague in hindsight, Sitney's discussion of Andy Warhol's *Sleep* (1963) offers a more concrete explanation. "Theorists such as [Stan] Brakhage and [Peter] Kubelka expounded the law that a film must not waste a frame and that a single film-maker must control all the functions of the creation," Sitney notes. "Warhol made the profligacy of footage the central fact of all of his early films, and he advertised his indifference to direction, photography, and lighting. He simply turned the camera on and walked away" (409–10). This latter idea—of Warhol's having simply "walked away" from the camera—resonates highly with *It's Impossible,* given that Linklater, as the sole filmmaker, frequently sets the camera on a tripod and walks away from the camera (though, unlike Warhol, for the purpose of performing). But aside from some basic similarities—the static camera shots that Linklater favors echo Warhol's aesthetic—the two films do not have much in common, given that Warhol's film is a six-hour view of a friend asleep, whereas Linklater's film actually presents a narrative, albeit an oblique one. A closer model for Linklater's approach might be James Benning, a filmmaker Linklater openly admires and has cited as an influence. Consider Barbara Pichler's and Benning's own description of *8½ x 11* (1974) (the internal quotation is Benning): "The project constitutes an experiment with narrative forms and possibilities of reception—film as a form of conceptual art which is not centered on story but instead focuses on image and structure while playing with narrative conventions, thus 'revealing the inadequecies [*sic*] of linear narrative and space'" (23). While Linklater's film has more interest in narrative than this description indicates, *It's Impossible* often explores the least amount of information a viewer can have while still experiencing the suggestion of character and plot, an impulse closely related to what Pichler and Benning describe. At times, for example, it is almost as though the film has been edited to include only transitions between scenes rather than the scenes themselves, approaching narrative legibility but never quite reaching it—and, again, contributing to a sense of waiting, the film's "profligacy" with narrative time, to appropriate Sitney's word, evident in the long stretches where nothing seems to happen and in the ellipses where something does.

A trip to Glacier National Park is telling. Since the film hints at the importance of Glacier earlier, when the protagonist indicates his desire to go there, viewers might expect the journey to assume some importance within the film, and a more traditional narrative might use the opportunity to develop exposition regarding the protagonist and secondary characters. Instead, the entire sequence, lasting just under two minutes, consists of four long shots:

1. A man and woman stand by a car, map in front of them, and discuss the locations of various lakes. Behind them, the protagonist loads up the trunk. (twenty-eight seconds)
2. The next morning, a campground fire smolders as someone leaves a tent in the background. (eleven seconds)
3. The protagonist brushes his teeth at a lake's edge, a vista in the background. (sixteen seconds)
4. Two men walk into the frame as we see another vista within the park itself. They linger at the road's edge as the protagonist kicks snow from his shoe (figure 1). (thirty-seven seconds)

Although the sequence includes dialogue, most of it does not, and even the dialogue that is audible is not always understandable. And while the arrival at Glacier provides a small sense of culmination, the next shot deflates any more lofty sensibilities, as we see the main character playing pinball, an activity that becomes a recurring motif in much of Linklater's work.

Figure 1. *It's Impossible to Learn to Plow by Reading Books*: the trip to Glacier.

This sequence is like so many others in the film, in that we rarely have a sense of the protagonist's interior life, whether at Glacier's edge or playing pinball, but instead must construct it based on very little evidence. Viewers may, for example, be momentarily baffled as to the significance of a scene later in Missoula, where he says good-bye to a woman we have seen briefly elsewhere, implying a romance that we can only imagine (subverted further by the odd camera placement at the top of a stairwell, blocking much of the exchange). Other oblique scenes provide glimpses of his interior life, but one of the most compelling ones comes quite late in the film. In a nod to the French New Wave—Linklater cites Godard's *Vivre sa vie* (1962) specifically ("Commentary—*It's Impossible*"), where Anna Karina's character watches Dreyer's *La Passion de Jeanne d'Arc* (1928)—the film depicts the director's alter ego watching another Dreyer film, *Gertrud* (1964), at the moment when Gertrud describes life as "a long . . . chain of dreams . . . drifting one into the other." Not only does this aptly capture the dreamlike pacing of this film, if not also anticipate the opening of *Slacker* and the whole of *Waking Life,* but it also underscores the intellectually curious figure of the protagonist himself, someone we have watched in a mundane present temporality—doing his laundry, feeding money into vending machine—much more than we have heard him engage in conversations, a reversal of typical character development. The light surprise of an early evening *Gertrud* screening, coming as it does with little warning, adds yet another layer to the character, even as it suggests a fundamental opacity in our ability to know him; moreover, it reiterates the inherent strangeness of the present moment, a running obsession throughout the film.

Although many scenes explore that obsession, the travel sequences take particular interest in it. Here, the simultaneously stimulating and dulling effects of displacement from home, combined with long periods of being inside a train, car, or other vehicle, make for boredom, to be sure, but seem also to open onto a sense of temporal awareness, where one feels time's passage as an almost material presence. So much of the film's exploration of this state occurs through its stylistic strategies. In long takes and relatively shorter ones (still much longer, it should be said, than most features), the editing often implies the promise of a narrative culmination but delays that promise, much as a travel destination might also, temporarily, remain beyond reach. Repetition, within these more montage-structured sequences, is an important part of that delay. The first train trip, for example, from Austin to Missoula, takes almost eight minutes of screen time and consists of twenty-two shots. Of those shots, six are repetitions of the protagonist walking through the train, often through one of the sliding doors, and seven of them are repetitions of the landscape passing by outside the window. In the former, the transitions rarely lead to any new activity on the part of the protagonist other than visiting a vending machine, eating, sleeping, or taking pills and brushing his teeth in a bathroom. The latter also rarely leads into any new scene and becomes instead a motif of passing landscapes. Other shots consist of the protagonist boarding and deboarding the train, and as the sequence builds, the viewer is encouraged to focus less on the protagonist's journey and more on the details of the film itself—the way a storm looks in the distance, outside of a window; the flashing red sign in a station where he stops at night; the mirrored windows of a highrise, reflecting another building; a tire yard amid utilitarian, decaying structures passing one by one. This, the film suggests, is how the travel experience, if not the present itself, actually is, in its material detail. Unlike other films, where characters might board a train only to step off of it seconds later, in a new city, this film lingers on the process of the journey itself, encouraging a mind-set of absorption in whatever the present moment offers. The final shot in the sequence, a shot outside of a window with raindrops streaking the glass in slow motion, suggests a deeply interior, almost meditative state that the protagonist has slipped into and that we, too, have been asked to experience. Such moments occur throughout the travel sequences, as in the next train trip, in a single shot, where a 7-Up can, a cup, and a candy bar on a tray table heave and sway to the rhythms of the train itself, so that the viewer is invited to experience the significantly slower pace of a form of transportation all but outmoded in contemporary America. Although Linklater will explore the experience of the present moment in much different ways in later films, one finds the seeds of such a preoccupation here in this early aesthetic experiment in boredom and beauty, as his protagonist simply walks out of the frame at the end and, seemingly, into his very next film, *Slacker.*

In the time following his making *It's Impossible to Learn to Plow by Reading Books,* Linklater continued living in Austin and helping to run the Austin Film Society. He tried unsuccessfully to make another feature, but when he could not secure funding for that project, he began thinking about a film that would combine several ideas he had culled through years of watching films, reading about them, and studying other texts—literature, philosophy, history—on his own. Linklater describes the moment he began putting together the film, in May 1989 (he would shoot the film that very summer): "After failing to get another film off the ground, I decide to burn all my credit, sell things, and call in every possible favor to do this movie that's been in my head for over five years. In one twenty-four hour period, I go through years of notebooks and material and assemble an outline for this movie that can be made with little resources in my own neighborhood. The energy is up around town and I can tell it will be a good summer to finally make this 'Austin movie'" (*Slacker* 3). Originally creating a "road map" in place of a more traditional script, Linklater penned general descriptions of scenes rather than line-by-line dialogue; the first scene, for example, reads, "As the sun is coming up, we see the skyline of Austin out a bus window. (Titles fill the dark area around the window)" (23). This approach left him open to the actors' own contributions as the project moved forward, and in general, a collaborative atmosphere infused the entire production. Its core group consisted of two of Linklater's friends from the Austin Film Society, Lee Daniel and Denise Montgomery, responsible for cinematography and sound (and Art Department), respectively; Clark Walker and Anne Walker-McBay (Walker as dolly grip and assistant camera; Walker-McBay as production manager and casting); Scott Rhodes, editor; Meg Brennan, script supervision; Debbie Pastor, also in the Art Department; and Linklater himself, involved in nearly every facet of the filmmaking process. Funding for the project came from a number of sources, including Linklater's Shell gas station card, which paid for crew meals. Shooting took place without the city's formal permission and led in part to the film's documentary qualities, as unknowing bystanders wandered in and out of the frame. In the months after the film's completion, *Slacker* saw little success before finding a very enthusiastic audience at the Seattle Film Festival in May 1990. But instead of that warm reception leading to national distribution, the film ran at the Dobie Theater in Austin for sold-out shows over the summer of 1990 before eventually being bought by Orion Classics. (Linklater's journal on this period, published in the St. Martin's Press *Slacker* book, has much more of this history, as does John Pierson's *Spike, Mike, Slackers & Dykes*, which notes a "substantive *Film Comment* piece"—an interview given at the Seattle Film Festival—that helped interest Orion Classics' Michael Barker [187].)

As this description indicates, *Slacker* embodies a narrative of independent filmmaking as eclectic creative act, performed on a small budget and outside of studio oversight, that nonetheless finds mainstream distribution. This narrative has been a powerful one for filmmakers, distributors, critics, and the popular imagination. Brian Price, in his 2003 profile on Linklater for the *Senses of Cinema* Great Directors Database, refers to the period in which *Slacker* was made as "the Rick Schmidt era of the American Independent film," a reference to Schmidt's 1989 book, *How to Make a Feature Film at Used Car Prices*. However influential Schmidt's book might have been, this idea of independent film production had already taken hold by 1991, as seen in an Associated

Press story titled "What Price the Off-Hollywood Shuffle?" (a reference to Robert Townsend's 1987 independent film, *Hollywood Shuffle*). Reflecting on *Slacker, Paris Is Burning,* and other recent works, Hillel Italie outlines "a typical, if optimistic, path" for such a film; although the article's dry tone indicates the difficulties in practice, his description illustrates a conception of independent cinema that continues to animate discussions today. "It's summer 1988 and you have a story idea," begins Italie matter-of-factly, before explaining the stages that follow, including funding ("You raise about 50,000 through credit cards and contributions from friends and relatives"), production and postproduction ("Filming lasts six weeks, but editing drags on and funds are low"), and the final moment of discovery and distribution ("Your work is accepted and receives a favorable response at Sundance"). While individual details differ between *Slacker* and Italie's description, the basic narratives are very close (no doubt *Slacker*'s history inflects Italie's more general ideas about "off-Hollywood"). That *Slacker* has held and continues to hold a place as a kind of watershed film at this moment in independent film history, both shaped by and helping to shape this conception of filmmaking, is perhaps why Linklater so often continues to be associated with independent cinema, despite a career that has seen numerous studio productions, beginning with *Dazed and Confused,* and despite his having critiqued, quite rightly, the idea of independent cinema as itself a signifier of quality (Koresky and Reichert).

Since its release, one of the most noted aspects of the film has been its unusual, almost nonexistent, narrative. In his 2007 *Me and You and Memento and Fargo: How Independent Screenplays Work,* J. J. Murphy speaks to the film's "semblance of narrative" that "presents enough bits of plot to tease the viewer into expecting greater narrative coherence than the film delivers" (247, 249). The description would seem to fit *It's Impossible* as well. But unlike that film, which follows a single protagonist's oblique, often wordless journey, this one follows multiple loquacious characters around a single town, Austin, as they appear and disappear quickly, moving from one to the next usually through what became known, for the filmmakers, as the "baton-pass" element of the film—usually, simply passing each other on the streets, one conversation continuing as another begins, transitioning through either camera movements or cuts (or both). Murphy argues that the multiple characters, drifting in and out of both frame and narrative, suggest an ensemble structure that the film plays with but never quite delivers, through what he refers to as the film's "dangling causes" (247). (Note that, following Murphy's lead, I have capitalized character names in what follows to avoid confusion for the reader, but they appear in their original form in this volume's filmography.) For example, Burglar reveals his name to be Paul during the failed robbery of the Old Anarchist's house, which recalls the "Paul" of the cryptic postcard farewell during the co-op scene (249). Like the gunshot of *It's Impossible,* Paul's "revelation," such as it is, leads nowhere, a "dangling cause" without effect. But despite the film's conveying a somewhat ambling attitude (as in Ultimate Loser's often quoted line, "Oh, I got some band practice in about five hours, so I figured I'd mosey on out"), *Slacker* actually effects these baton passes rapidly and smoothly, so that viewers experience a surprisingly large number of potential narratives within the film's one hundred minutes—twenty-seven, at least, or on average one every four minutes. Because characters and locations sometimes carry over, however, that number might actually be lower or higher, depending upon the individual viewer. For instance, when the four women in the bar meet Steve, and Steve drives them to the club, both scenes may be part of the same narrative—since they both involve Steve—or may be discrete, since he shows up only after the first scene has been ongoing for some time, and leaves quickly once they reach the club, the film now more interested in the two women riding bicycles to another show (which, again, may or may not include Steve's narrative, too). *Slacker's* unwillingness to draw neat, manageable story lines ties into its larger ethos of narrative experimentation and, like many of its characters, is content to let us dwell in our questions.

In addition to its unusual narrative, *Slacker's* style has also been frequently remarked upon. Jon Radwan, for example, has discussed the "non-intrusive and nonjudgmental" camerawork, the casting of nonactors, and other stylistic tendencies (38–41). Deriving largely from the cinematic modernisms since the Second World War, the neorealisms and new waves that have taken their cameras into the streets, time and time again, *Slacker* mixes its amorphous plotting with a quasi-documentary sensibility, the contingencies of production imbuing dialogue and narrative with a sense of unpredictability. Take, for example, the film's most famous scene, where Ultimate Loser and Stephanie from Dallas encounter Pap Smear Pusher, whose image would become the primary icon of the film itself, adorning posters, early videotapes of the film, and even the most recent Criterion DVD release (figure 2). As Pap Smear Pusher lives up to her character's name ("This—this will blow your gourd"), the scene calls attention to its profilmic reality—that is, the reality of the actual time and space when the scene was shot—through the camera's constant reframing, which allows viewers to take in the background as well as the foreground, and even more so with the performance style. The nonprofessional actors seem genuinely uncomfortable in ways that go beyond the characters they are playing, particularly at the outset of the scene, where Ultimate Loser and Stephanie from Dallas make little eye contact and engage in nervous behavior (for Ultimate Loser, playing with his fingernails; for Stephanie from Dallas, not quite knowing what to do with the sunglasses in her hands). Also, while the mise-en-scène's verisimilitude lends it a certain amount of realism—the alley, the graffiti motif of the hand, the beer bottles on the ground and stairs—sound

Figure 2. Pap Smear Pusher talks to Ultimate Loser and Stephanie from Dallas in *Slacker*'s iconic scene.

creates an even greater sense of the reality that exists outside the frame. Cars pass, engines rising without regard to the dialogue, and the sounds of birds, although pleasant, are not what one might associate with an alley in a narrative film, "unmotivated" by the set itself. As it has aged, *Slacker* has also taken on another documentary function, in serving as an archive of Austin music in the late 1980s. Pap Smear Pusher is played by Teresa Taylor, a drummer for the band probably most well known nationally from the Austin scene at this time, the Butthole Surfers (their song "Strangers Die Everyday" accompanies the credit sequence). Ultimate Loser and Stephanie from Dallas are Scott Marcus and Stella Weir, respectively; both were members of a popular Austin band, Glass Eye. And several other musicians either play songs (the bands Triangle Mallet Apron and Ed Hall) or act (Kathy McCarty, of Glass Eye, or Frank Orrall and Abra Moore, of Poi Dog Pondering). More broadly, the film makes its desire for a hybrid of narrative and documentary elements explicit in its final legal disclaimer, an inversion of the typical wording: "This story was based on fact. Any similarity with fictional events or characters is entirely coincidental."

These aspects—the unusual narrative, the documentary approach—set up this film's own temporal investigations, which are not entirely different from Linklater's previous film. But in contrast to *It's Impossible,* where we experience a sense of the present through a character who reveals little about himself, allowing the mundane details of travel to assume the foreground, in *Slacker* we are presented with a decentralized narrative of multiple characters who exteriorize their intellectual obsessions. They have active, curious minds, ones that seek to provoke discussion and debate through long deliveries of their ideas rather than a back-and-forth conversation. Although this seems selfish and, at times, probably is, it also illustrates an overwhelming sense of creative energy in its most raw state, largely through the long, unbroken monologue. The ephemeral orality of arguments, reflections, rants, and other hypotheses both plausible and absurd—sometimes both—becomes, in its own way, a celebration of the present moment, since these monologues are lost the second they are spoken and since, in their dynamism, they would not appear quite the same even if the speaker were asked to repeat the ideas again. They convey immediacy, obsessions spilling out into the present moment like jazz riffs, scat singing in a spoken-word poetry of its own rhythms, so that giving them voice becomes a process of discovery not just for viewer and on-screen listener but for the speaker his- or herself as well. And the film rarely privileges any one character's views over the other. "Conspiracy A-Go-Go" Author's theories on the Kennedy assassinations have as much interest as Video Backpacker's views on media, and both have no more or less interest than Old Anarchist's embellished self-history. Even a character such as Traumatized Yacht Owner is allowed to deliver her own ideas, and although there is a certain humor to the absurdity of events that Happy-Go-Lucky Guy experiences, there is also an investment in these moments that offers them up as valid, even at their most strange. Without a clear narrative destination in mind, like *It's Impossible*, the viewer is encouraged to dwell in the particulars; the film posits the present moment as something unpredictable, one constantly unfolding, containing, even at its most absurd, a certain degree of mystery. "The necessary beauty in life is in giving yourself to it completely. Only later will it clarify itself and become coherent," speaks Old Man Recording Thoughts into His Microphone. This present-centered ethos, even if promising a clarity set in the future, informs the verbiage that tumbles from character to character, scene to scene, allowing that we may be confused in places, but that such confusion is okay by *Slacker*, too.

As a brief digression—which seems appropriate, given this film—we might also consider the context of a college town (one Murphy also notes), where residents, particularly in their twenties and thirties, are at various stages of education, particularly one devoted to the humanities. For all of its talk of more discussion-based pedagogy and student-centered approach, the academy is still very much a lecture-driven environment in which professors are encouraged to communicate course material via uninterrupted speech, and at scholarly conferences, the traditional format of presentations, still widely practiced, is to read an essay aloud that one has already written ahead of time. It is as though these characters have absorbed this sensibility into their own conversations and applied it to subjects the academy might not normally treat—or might very well treat, such as in the ideological discussion of *The Smurfs* or the relationship between memory and the televised image (as in Video Backpacker's recollection of witnessing a violent crime and being unable to "pause" the image or "adjust the hue").

Regardless of the college-town context, the steady stream of monologues only makes the ending that much more cathartic, in the final
Super-8 footage of four friends who head up to an overlook (Mount
Bonnell, for those familiar with Austin) and eventually throw the camera
itself over the edge, in the ultimate rejection of any one authority, including the filmmaker's. This self-referential moment is the culmination
of similar acknowledgments throughout the film of its own materiality,
such as Hit-and-Run Son's playing the childhood film before the police
arrive, Recluse in Bathrobe and Shut-in Girlfriend's watching television,
the student interview with Hitchhiker Awaiting "True Call," the Video
Backpacker, and the Pixelvision sequence. Furthermore, Linklater acknowledges the style and structure of the film in other ways, as in Having a Breakthrough Day's use of the Oblique Strategies cards, an actual
deck designed originally by Brian Eno and Peter Schmidt in order to
provoke new thinking about a given aesthetic project when one feels
a conceptual dead-end has been reached. "It's not building a wall but
making a brick," one card reads, an acknowledgment of the interest in
individual scenes rather than the whole; likewise, the card that reads
"Repetition is a form of change," when the women are at the bar, not
only humorously reflects on the repetitive nature of the service industry,
since this is the card the waiter receives, but also encourages viewers to
think anew about the structural commonalities among the scenes. Given
the many references to the film's making in ways both obvious and less
so, one might begin to think about *Slacker* as an investigation of the
moments leading up to a finished aesthetic work, ideas and sketches
that might eventually become their own separate, more "finished" cre-
ations but that also have a satisfying existence in their own right. In this
way, Linklater and company pay tribute to those moments in aesthetic
creation that often go unnoticed—ideas recorded on cocktail napkins or
in journals, or even more fleetingly, those that pass through the writer's
mind but never make it to the page or, in making it to the page, become
diminished, less strange and often less interesting. One thinks of Allen
Ginsberg's reflections in *Howl* of those "who scribbled all night rocking
and rolling over lofty incantations which in the yellow morning were
stanzas of gibberish" (16). *Slacker* is an ode to films, books, and other
creative works in their nascent state, the present moment of journal
entries and "scribbling" in which they arrive, and the acknowledgment

that, although they may inform one's later work, they might equally be abandoned, like Ginsberg's "gibberish," which makes the final creative act so appropriate, as the film pitches itself over a cliff.

Just as *Slacker* began with a direct link to *It's Impossible* in Should Have Stayed at the Bus Station's monologue, its ending with four young people driving around town in the early hours, so clearly having a wonderful time, points to the subject of Linklater's next film, *Dazed and Confused*. In a 1993 publication tie-in for the film, he describes how the film originated with a song: "About six years ago, I was driving along and heard an early ZZ Top song from their legendary 'Fandango' album. I flashed to a 1976 night piled in a LeMans with three others, listening to the 'Fandango' 8-track. I remembered how it clicked over from track to track all night long, and we drove around endlessly, looking for something to happen. . . . At the end of the evening we had driven almost 150 miles and of course, had gotten nowhere" (*Dazed and Confused* 5). The timing of this initiating memory would have fallen before he had begun shooting *Slacker*, but it was not until *Slacker*'s promotional tour that he would first discuss the idea publicly, in an interview with Gary Arnold (Pierson 196). Arnold passed along this project to Jim Jacks, who, with Sean Daniels, had a deal with Universal Pictures; Alphaville Productions, their production company, was named after a Godard film, a no doubt attractive quality for a cinephile like Linklater (Black, "Take Two"). Linklater's "teenage rock and roll film," sold by Jacks and Daniels to Universal as "an updated *American Graffiti*," would be his first studio film, with a budget of $6.9 million (Spong). In June 1992, almost three years after he had begun production on *Slacker*, Linklater would shoot *Dazed* in the same place, and the experience, as he has since recounted it in interviews and commentaries, was not an altogether pleasant one. Working with a larger crew presented some initial difficulties, and Linklater frequently had disagreements with the studio over any number of issues, none perhaps more so than the soundtrack, where he did not want new bands doing covers of older songs, as opposed to getting the actual songs (which they eventually did, on what would be a very profitable soundtrack). When the film opened, it played on 183 screens, to the director's disappointment, and made about $8 million, though its popularity on cable, video, and DVD would make it very profitable in the years to come. In 2003 its earnings had reached $30 million, a figure that has no doubt risen and will continue to do so, as new generations discover Pink, Mitch, and company's day, night, and day in 1976 (Spong). *Dazed*'s genesis from a song, which set off that initial set of memories for Linklater, raises the concept of nostalgia more generally, an attitude that appeals to many people but one that has been frequently criticized in scholarly writings of the late twentieth and early twenty-first centuries, nowhere more famously than in Fredric Jameson's theoretical treatise *Postmodernism, or, The Cultural Logic of Late Capitalism.* Jameson identified *American Graffiti*, an important precursor for *Dazed*, as the first "nostalgia film," a genre that, for Jameson, reimagines early time periods through a kind of "mesmerizing lost reality," one that damages our sense of both the present and the past (19). While discussing another nostalgia film, *Body Heat* (1981), Jameson describes how it "endows present reality and the openness of present history with the spell and distance of a glossy mirage" (21). For Jameson, such estrangement from one's own present, enabled by the experience of the nostalgia film, has negative repercussions for us culturally, since we become more complacent—and less politically aware—as a result. Given its often powerful effects on memory, music can enact that "mesmerizing lost reality" even further; David R. Shumway, working in light of Jameson's arguments, has noted that soundtracks in the nostalgia film "creat[e] a fictional set of memories that . . . may actually come to replace the audience's 'original' sense of the past" (40). The sense of "fictional" memories resonates highly with *Dazed*, given that many of its most ardent fans were too young to be alive during the period actually depicted, much as Shumway observes with the original audiences for *American Graffiti*. Even if, however, audiences find their own sense of nostalgia in *Dazed*, they may find it quickly undercut by several factors. For one, the soundtrack is much more specific than many other nostalgia films; Linklater was careful, for example, not to use any songs that might have been released in June 1976, a month after the setting for the film. For another, the film self-consciously recognizes its own characters' nostalgia, such as Cynthia's discussion of previous decades, when she imagines that the 1980s "will be radical," or the earlier nostalgia brainstorm by the students at school, immediately thrown into self-conscious relief by the women's musings on the sexist implications of *Gilligan's Island* (1964–1967). Even more broadly, the film's explicit depictions of the more bleak aspects of high school life—the physical and mental humiliations that several characters endure—make any overly nostalgic reactions almost absurd. (Lesley Speed also has offered a compelling case against nostalgic readings of *Dazed,* focusing on the themes of "immediacy" and "transition," in the essay "Tuesday's Gone.") But *Dazed* certainly explores the past, not only through the history of the period, such as in references to the bicentennial both sincere and ironic in nature, but also in its self-consciousness about the genre to which it belongs: the teenpic.

Even more than its studio context, *Dazed's* working within an identifiable genre represents a break from Linklater's previous two films, notwithstanding the road-film elements to *It's Impossible.* One of the most popular of contemporary genres, the teenpic, according to Steve Neale's *Genre and Hollywood,* has been a strong component of mainstream filmmaking since at least the postwar period, in examples ranging from the relatively serious approach of *Rebel without a Cause* (1955) to lighter fare such as the American Independent Pictures beach films of the 1960s (120–21). Within that tradition, *Dazed* also draws on two subgenres identified by Neale—the rock-and-roll film and the hot-rod film. Examples of the former include "*Shake, Rattle, and Rock* (1956) and *Rock, Rock, Rock!* (1956)" and, for the latter, "*Dragstrip Riot* (1958) and *Hot-Rod Girl* (1956)" (121–22). Certainly, one need only think of both the opening and the closing of *Dazed* to see this generic fusion in sound and image: the film begins with Aerosmith's "Sweet Emotion," combined with Pickford's Pontiac GTO "Judge," and ends with Foghat's "Slow Ride," combined with Wooderson's Chevy Chevelle "Super Sport." Its debt to *American Graffiti,* another teenpic that draws on both subgenres, is readily apparent in both scenes. (For an excellent exploration of many subjects under discussion here, including nostalgia and genre, in light of pastiche, see Mary Harrod's article "The Aesthetics of Pastiche in the Work of Richard Linklater.") But *Dazed's* narrative structure draws on the teenpic in larger ways, particularly when setting up its larger designs in the opening. After a fairly standard credit sequence, the film's opening ten minutes introduce several common markers of the genre, including an adolescent, male protagonist, Pink; a central social event, Pickford's party; a central conflict, the drug-free pledge; and secondary plots common to the teenpic, including a romantic subplot (Pink and Simone) and one related to the awkwardness of the freshman experience (in this case, the hazing of the junior high students). As it moves forward, however, the film will dismantle nearly all of these aspects: the film adds a protagonist, Mitch, splitting the narrative in two; the social event, Pickford's party, will be canceled (though arguably replaced by the Moon Tower); the central conflict will occupy few of the characters' discussions, though it remains important; the romantic subplot will be almost beside the point, since Simone appears little and Pink's interactions with Jodi are minimal (if any couples get nods to the more traditional romantic subplot, they are Mitch and Julie, Tony and Sabrina, and even, albeit humorously, Wooderson and Cynthia); and the awkwardness of the freshman experience—and hazing—are undercut by the ways that both Mitch and Sabrina accompany the seniors throughout the evening. O'Bannion, the "villain" of the film, if there is one, exits quite early, and even Sabrina's final encounter with Darla is not finally the point. In this way, *Dazed* establishes a narrative end only to resist it by allowing for a much more meandering pace, one in keeping with an attitude that looks on the present moment as having an intrinsic value in and of itself. And one of the most important ways the film celebrates that value is through creative, active engagement with something we so often take for granted: our language.

From its opening conversations outside of school, *Dazed* explores the ways adolescents use, bend, and shape language, particularly in the way it unfolds in the present almost musically, much like the jazz-inflected riffs of *Slacker*'s various declaimers. Just as Eric Rohmer's films might be thought of as documents of speech, whether of a certain class (the bourgeois intellectual) or a given actor (Rohmer was so attentive to his actors' own language that he famously claimed not to understand lines he had appropriated for the script of *La Collectionneuse* [1967] [Monaco 303]), *Dazed and Confused* attempts to capture the rhythms of late-twentieth-century adolescent speech, at once both inventive and derivative (and, in its derivative qualities, often enormously creative). Part of the reason for this accuracy in language is undoubtedly because, like Rohmer, Linklater listens to the language his actors use when not in character; he also allows for collaboration with them, most significantly in the *Before* films, in which actors share screenwriting credits, but also in his other work (and most certainly in this film, as he relates in the interview of this volume). In *Dazed* Linklater avoids the pitfalls of so many teenpics, which tend either to give adolescents lines that sound like people twice their age *or* to make the opposite error and presume a teenage character does not have a complex interior life. *Dazed* does neither—instead, it offers us a sense of the ways language is put to use by teens themselves.

One of those ways is the repeated phrase, which serves to define the individual and to connect people socially. Slater's "That's what I'm talking about" or Wooderson's "Alright" (or "Alright, alright, alright") for example, both define each character as he wants to be seen by the world, even if, in Slater's case, at least, it also reveals something more about him—an ironic acknowledgment that, while *he* may know what he is talking about, we may not. Such phrases belong to the past, in the sense that they have been said many times before, based on the reactions of those who hear them; that said, they exist in the present moments, when characters connect and reconnect with one other, whether passing each other in the halls of school, driving around town, or meeting at a late-night, improvised social setting. Language thus serves a communal function, and these connections extend outward from the characters to the audience (it is small wonder that these lines tend to be those most repeated by viewers). And just as these exchanges occur in the present, language also acts as a constantly updated, dynamic oral history. O'Bannion's confrontation with Carl's mother, Mitch's getting busted at the baseball game, and the angry mailbox owner's confrontation with the guys in Pickford's car are all three events we see retold shortly after they have happened. While David Bordwell has shown that redundancy serves narrative functions within Hollywood cinema (77–82), in *Dazed* the redundancy underscores and even celebrates an essential boredom, one that leaves open a certain degree of freedom within the present moment, even if these characters are anything but free, the expectations of school and community lightly though no less importantly made explicit throughout the film. (Mike and Tony's commenting on the absurdity of selling concessions while the senior girls haze the incoming freshmen is one of many such acknowledgments.) In fact, it is only here, within language itself, where such expectations might be resisted, in a linguistic energy of the present moment, one that the film looks upon with real affection, even if it disapproves of many of its speakers' actions. As a side note, at least one other important aspect of the specificity of *Dazed*'s language exists in the subtle but distinct differences between the language of the junior high students and that of their senior high counterparts; the former's lack of sophistication manifests itself in their diction (words like *pissant*), their inflections (the overexaggerated, clumsy sarcasm), and in their frequent inability to articulate anything at all. This is particularly true with Mitch's character, and viewers who mock Wiley Wiggins for his uncomfortable gestures (touching his nose, for example) and awkward pauses are missing the point—yes, these may be the articulations of a first-time actor, but part of why they work so well is that the uncomfortable gestures of an amateur performer correspond to the fumbling self-consciousness of a character moving from early to late adolescence (just as, in *Slacker*, the awkwardness of the nonprofessional actors worked to that film's favor in other ways). Yet again this serves only toward establishing a greater specificity with these characters, so that all adolescents are not lumped into one group and the subtle distinctions that adolescents themselves draw are made clear (as when Mitch asks, "Hey man, what grade's she in?").

This life stage, in fact—adolescence—is where *Dazed* most greatly explores at a thematic level its investment in a sense of present-ness, enabled by the combination of generic detours—one almost cannot help using the word when writing about Linklater's films—language, and, of course, style. Lee Daniel's wide-screen compositions render the social space as static, where events unfold slowly and, for the most part, without fanfare, even when a great deal seems to be happening, as with the Moon Tower party. This approach begins in the high school, in the opening of the film, as in the shot where Pink, Pickford, and Michelle run into Slater by the water fountain. The camera trails slowly after them, moving around as they talk to one another, and lingers on the stoned Uncle Sam mural behind them after the conversation is over; the angle and staging block any early view of the painting so that the visual joke will be more effective at its end. Another even more representative moment is when Pink talks about the pledge with Cynthia, Mike, and Tony in a single take; the take itself is actually longer, beginning with Shavonne, Kaye, and Jodi and continuing the "baton-pass" element of *Slacker*, albeit in a more muted way. The camera faces the characters as they talk to Pink (figure 3). Behind them, a student leans against the chalkboard; another walks through the background at a slow pace. Although narratively the

Figure 3. Cinematography in
Dazed and Confused.

scene sets up some tension regarding the through-line of Pink's pledge
(will he sign?), visually, nothing appears to be happening, an appropriate
depiction, since the last days of most schools are usually perfunctory,
students and teachers both having completed their work and killing time
before summer begins. And while the stylistic choices will become more
dynamic in later scenes—crane shots, slow motion, zoom-ins, and other
techniques—the essential approach of long, wide-screen compositions,
actors almost facing the camera, appears and reappears throughout the
film and at nearly every location, including the multiple car conversations, shot from the hood and facing the occupants directly. This motif
within the cinematography connects all of the later scenes to that essential sense of boredom established in the lingering hours of a last day of
high school. Yet within that sense of boredom, characters are given the
room to enjoy themselves, with the film's rising to occasional euphoric
moments within that larger sensibility, mostly through Mitch, for whom
everything is new—the early-morning rendezvous with Julie set to Seals
and Crofts's "Summer Breeze," as they break into laughter, is one of
the film's most purely joyful moments. All of this occurs within a narrative structured with a destination—Pink's pledge—but taking delight in
resisting that destination as long as possible, in an ethos that celebrates
the present moment for what it is, whether blissful or boring (the two

by no means exclusive in *Dazed*). As time stalls, so do we, but the film is no less pleasurable as a result, whether in the inherently inactive periods of the last day of school, the baseball game (a sport often characterized, fairly or not, by periods of inactivity), the car rides around town, the gatherings at the Emporium and the Moon Tower, the fifty-yard-line joint, and Mitch's collapsing on his bed as the group in Wooderson's car heads out of town. Such drift (narrative, generic, stylistic) enables an ode to the conversation as creative activity produced while hanging out and, even more, celebrates a desire to be attentive to the present, despite the anxieties of characters about the immediate past (Mike's obsessing over Cliff's antagonisms) or the future (Mike's wondering what people will say about the fight later). Cynthia captures this ironic temporal juxtaposition well when she says she would like to stop "thinking about the present, right now, as some minor insignificant preamble to something else," and this is very much the film's desire as well, as the characters leave us to pursue their goal for the summer, Aerosmith tickets, to be purchased at a destination where they will presumably once again engage in another boring activity (likely made fun, given the company): waiting in line.

Explorations of temporality would continue to inflect the narratives of Linklater's next three features: twenty-four hours in Vienna, a night in "Burnfield," and a few years in early-twentieth-century America, in *Before Sunrise, subUrbia,* and *The Newton Boys,* respectively.

A Brief Encounter, the Road to Burnfield, and One Hell of a Way to Make a Living

Cinephilia is often characterized by a tendency to privilege fragments over the whole, particularly with individual moments in a film that take on even more charged meaning in the personal response of the viewer. (Some scholars have even suggested using such moments as ways of avoiding entrenched academic approaches to film analysis.) Memory, too, plays a role in this subjective privileging of fragments, perhaps in part because cinema has itself trained us to imagine our memories in this way, as a montage of images and sounds that exist impressionistically, in fleeting transitions between scenes or in heightened sequences that haunt the protagonist. With *Before Sunrise,* my own admittedly subjective moment comes near the beginning of the film, after Celine and Jesse have met on the train and Jesse has convinced Celine to accompany him in Vienna until his plane leaves the following morning. As they leave the train, Jesse steps off and walks out of the frame, but Celine lingers on the steps of the train as the camera tracks from right to left. She dips her head, and we see a small smile cross her face, as she hesitates there. It is a small delay, but in that moment, Celine pulls the film to a stop, briefly, since both Jesse and we need her to get off the train if anything is going to happen in the next twenty-four hours, in Jesse's case, and the next eighty minutes, in ours. And so, she steps off the train, following a man whose name she does not yet even know into the streets of Vienna. Although I am sure other viewers enjoy this moment as well, it is also true that my response here is elevated, subjectively and personally. To be sure, this film tends to draw very personal responses from writers, ones where the critical and the personal seem to merge (or at least are not treated as exclusive of one another). For example, Robin Wood's "Rethinking Romantic Love: *Before Sunrise*" opens with, "I knew, the first time I saw *Before Sunrise* (1995), that here was a film for which I felt not only interest or admiration but love" (*Sexual Politics and Narrative Film* 318), and Erik Syngle's "Love Me Tonight" begins, "We can choose the films we like, but the films we love tend to choose us, slip quietly into our lives until we look up one day and are shocked to realize there was ever a time before we knew them." While Glen Norton's article "The Seductive Slack of *Before Sunrise*" does not begin with such a straightforward admission, by its end, he confesses, "*Before Sunrise* is a film that affects one's consciousness, remaining there long after the last images have faded from the screen. An attempt at objective criticism would imply a denial of these feelings" (72). Of course, these descriptions apply equally to Celine and Jesse's own sentiments, and Robin Wood ends his essay by making this connection explicit, where he compares the lovers' "attempt to bridge 'this little space in between'" (referencing Celine's speculations on the divine) to "the critic's relationship to the films she/he loves" (335). In this film, romantic love, cinephilia, and love for life itself are ultimately inseparable (lest we be overwhelmed, Kathy McCarty's cover of Daniel Johnston's "Living Life" reassures us over the closing credits that "everything's all right").

In the sequel to this film, *Before Sunset*, Celine remarks to Jesse, "Maybe we are . . . only good at brief encounters walking around in

European cities in [a] warm climate." Celine's observation calls to mind David Lean's 1945 *Brief Encounter*, an adaptation of Noël Coward's *Still Life* (part of the larger *Tonight at 8.30* series) and a connection many reviewers referenced when *Before Sunset* was released. Coward's play and Lean's film famously dramatize two married people, Alec and Laura, meeting in the refreshment room of a train station, carrying on a romance over roughly a year's time, and eventually departing one another for good, when a blithely obtuse friend of Laura's unwittingly prevents any closure in the final moments as Alec catches his train (on his last trip, before heading to Africa). The details share little in common with *Before Sunrise*, which takes place over roughly twenty-four hours between two people who are not in other relationships and whose only seeming obstacle for their remaining together is geography. Yet the accidental meeting (in a train, no less), the fragility and intensity of their innate connection, along with the deadline of a train's departure cannot help but recall Alec and Laura's own small meetings over tea in the few minutes before their trains go separate ways. Most crucial here is the powerful connection that both couples share and that viewers must be willing to accept if the narrative is to work at all. In this respect, *Before Sunrise* recalls an even more important precursor, Agnès Varda's 1962 *Cléo de 5 à 7*—in particular, the final act of the film, where Cléo meets Antoine, a young soldier on leave from the Algerian War, and shares an innate connection with him, one crystallized in the fine final moments of the film, in a look shared between the two actors so sublime that Varda later failed to duplicate in reshoots. In *Remembrances*, an essay-film available on the Criterion Collection's box set of her films, Varda notes of this experience (here, I rely on the English subtitles), "You can't just try to recapture something so ephemeral and miraculous. What a lesson." One could apply the same lesson to *Before Sunrise* itself, in the specificity of its own moments and in the particularity of Celine and Jesse's innate connection.

In fact, Celine's word choice here of the "encounter" resonates with Varda's own discussions about *Cléo*. Speaking on the film in 1962, she noted,

At that time, the fashion consisted in saying there wasn't any possible communication. . . . It's a notion that Antonioni cultivated fervently,

Resnais as well. . . . I don't agree. . . . I believe in "encounters." According to their possibilities, people meet for an instant, a minute, or a lifetime. They have one encounter or ten in their existence, or they don't have any. But everyone, one way or another, needs it. Those who know it are already less unhappy than those who don't. . . . This need is essential. It must be said in an almost primary way, because it's very important. (qtd. Sellier 219)

This need is what Varda's final act explores, as Cléo and Antoine meet in a park, take a bus trip, and eventually end up at the hospital where Cléo receives the ambiguous news that she does indeed have cancer—but that it can be treated. In addition to its devoting the entire film to what Varda describes, *Before Sunrise* echoes the director's work in one of the most stylistically daring moments of the whole film, a roughly six-minute single take on a streetcar that recalls the long bus trip of *Cléo's* final act (figure 4). (The tracks of the streetcar fall between the two, which also evokes the unintended detail of *Cléo's* final shot.) Like most of the conversations in *Before Sunrise,* the dialogue here has an organic quality, shifting easily among divergent topics—their first sexual desires (Jesse affecting a Freudian accent appropriate for the Viennese setting), politics, media culture, even souls and the afterlife—and the camera

Figure 4. The long take on the streetcar
in *Before Sunrise.*

captures these exchanges in a two-shot where we are invited to watch both speaker and listener at once. Although the entire film might be said to embody Godard's famous description of *Breathless* as a documentary of its actors, this scene blurs the distinction between character and performer particularly well. Small gestures become more noticeable, such as when Celine looks down as she describes a boy who asked her out at summer camp, or Jesse's starting to sweep her hair from her face, then hesitating—because she has looked up, or because that is too familiar, too intimate, for this early moment in their twenty-four-hour time together. *Before Sunrise* here immerses us in the present moment, even as they discuss their past, and this immersion and accompanying interest in body language will be explored again in the scene that follows, in one of the other more stylistic daring moments of the film, a shared record-booth experience as the two exchange looks over Kath Bloom's "Come Here."

In the published script of *Before Sunrise*, Celine asks Jesse, as they are suspended in the Ferris wheel, "How come every time you want me to do something, you start talking about time travel?" Jesse has just proposed that the two "jump in time" to the inevitable kiss they will later share so as to take advantage of a stunning sunset and a Ferris-wheel encounter (46); in the actual film, the scene loses this dialogue in favor of a more intuitive, tender moment between the lovers, though the time-travel reference appears earlier, when Jesse first convinces Celine to leave the train. Although much can be said about time in Linklater's films, if not cinema more generally, *Before Sunrise* and *Before Sunset* are two of the most explicitly fascinated films in this regard in Linklater's entire body of work. In relation to the latter, he has noted, "I really just wanted to capture two people existing. And let the context take care of itself. Time and cinema. Tarkovsky put it so eloquently in his book *Sculpting in Time*. He articulates it as well as anyone, cinema's particular relation to time. . . . I guess my idea of storytelling drifts in that direction" (Koresky and Reichert). In this *Before Sunrise* shares yet another connection with *Cléo*, in relation to an explicit interest in time—that is, that one's phenomenological experience of time is often quite different, more subjective, far more rich and strange, than the time of the clock—yet it is the clock's time that moves us forward, for Jesse and Celine, for Hawke and Delpy, and for the audience. "You cannot conquer time," Jesse reminds us, imitating Dylan Thomas's reading of

W. H. Auden's "As I Walked Out One Evening" in a scene late in the film where these characters, too, cannot halt their departures (and, for Auden, for Cléo, and for these two, death itself). But time can be bent—at least, subjectively—swayed by the present tense of a moment that lingers or, conversely, by the conscious examination of temporality itself. This latter strategy is one the lovers engage in frequently, as if one's self-awareness of time might temporarily provide relief from Auden's relentless clocks—or, even, might shape an alternative time zone the lovers might inhabit, however briefly. In a long take of the two on a large marble rail, looking down at one of the intersections in Vienna, the surrounding buildings lit up, Jesse remarks, "I feel like this is some dream world we're in, you know?" to which Celine responds, "Yeah, it's so weird. It's like our time together is just ours. It's our own creation. It must be like I'm in your dream and you're in mine." The experience of time as a self-aware dream, or a waking dream, appears elsewhere in the film, particularly in one of the key moments when Celine confesses that "I always have this strange feeling that I'm this very old woman, laying down, about to die—you know, that my life is just her memories or something." If we follow Celine's logic, then the film itself is this woman's dream, and—why not?—we are too, wherever we are when we see it. The audience is thus complicit in this push-and-pull of time's moving forward and time's delay, and although we cannot conquer time, either, we can enjoy the space that these lovers create, dream or not, and even help in its shaping, as they "encounter" one another in Varda's sense of the word.

Jesse and Celine's reflections on time join other subjects as well—death, particularly in light of Auden, but also religion, art, music, politics, gender, relationships, and other topics. Recall that Celine and Jesse's initial meeting occurs over reading, with their holding books by Georges Bataille and Klaus Kinski. (One need only try to imagine what it would be like to see either text in the hands of one's fellow traveling companions, much less two people sitting across from one another, to have a sense of the star-crossed dynamic at work in the script.) But beyond that, these references from the outset make it clear that this film is not just about a romantic encounter, however brief; it is as much a celebration of the life of the mind—of two minds, really, an intellectual harmony as important as the romantic and spiritual ones also shared by the central couple. (The literary reference of the date, Bloomsday, also underscores this intellectual harmony.) Note that, for however many subjects both characters reflect upon, neither one of them mentions a college course where they might have studied them, nor do either of them exchange much information about universities attended. What matters here is not so much knowledge accrued as curiosity itself—or that knowledge is good only insofar as it feeds into such curiosity. Consider the moment when they see the posters for the exhibit of Georges Seurat drawings; this brief scene begins about halfway into the film. The advertisements are for the same show, but each poster has a different image, four in all. Celine and Jesse stop to admire the posters, Celine leading Jesse—and us—through each one. Rather than reflect on Seurat's history or aesthetic criticism, she instead recalls the intense experience of first seeing them—the way, for example, she stared at one for forty-five minutes. This experience is echoed briefly here, in the way that the camera frames each sketch as Celine talks about it, her finger pointing to it, actually touching it, in that gesture that people often long to enact themselves when in a museum, Celine's violation of the taboo confirming Walter Benjamin's famous arguments about the aura of art in the age of mechanical reproduction even as the same gesture ironically underscores that aura exponentially. All the while, Jesse is here silent; it is noteworthy that both characters will allow the other to speak for long stretches, indicating the importance of listening as well as speaking in this life of the mind—that both are important to intellectual exchange. And in framing each image in close-up, with Celine's off-screen voice leading us through them, the film encourages us to take part in this exchange as well, to make our own discoveries, wherever we may find them, and to remain open and curious to the encounter with art, both those in a traditional museum context (the one advertised in the poster) and in a more nontraditional place (in a public advertisement context, if not wherever the viewer his or herself happens to be while watching the film, whether in the multiplex, the home, or some other space). Such openness and curiosity, while it may build on the knowledge gained through past experience, are very much about being alert to the present moment and how learning only continues to inflect the lives of those who take it seriously. The most nakedly romantic, if not equally radical, notion of the entire film might be not that two people make such an intense connection in a span of about twenty-four hours but that an open curiosity to learning should neither be ironically dismissed nor be subsumed by erudition itself but that it should be embraced with the optimism and joy found here. These ideas and so many others reverberate in the lovely final montage, moving across the city and the various locations visited by the lovers, as though Vienna itself will carry their memory rather than the reverse—Celine boarding her train and Jesse, his bus, en route to the plane that will return him to the States.

When Jesse's plane lands, however, we may wish to seek a return ticket—or, at the very least, to continue driving as we pass through Burnfield, the setting for Linklater's next film, a dark adaptation of Eric Bogosian's play *subUrbia*. The opening credits are a reversal of *Before Sunrise*'s closing montage; whereas the latter captured aesthetically pleasing locations still resonating with romantic desire, this sequence foregrounds ugliness. Many shots depict nearly empty parking lots in front of strip malls, such as one showing the decaying, broken pavement stretching outward from a PetSmart; Gene Pitney's accompanying song, "Town without Pity," reminds us that while this community may draw upon our sympathies, such sentiment is one-way only. Other shots reveal identical rows of apartment buildings, townhouses, driveways, and drainage ditches between subdivisions; the cumulative effect recalls a passage from Bogosian's introduction to the film's screenplay, where he describes his own hometown of Woburn, Massachusetts, the play's thinly veiled setting, as "a patchwork of stately turn-of-the-century homes, industrial waste sites, subdivisions built over old farms, freeways, and strip malls" (*subUrbia* [screenplay] 1). The cinematography moves from right to left, outside of a car window, except for the end, where it shifts from left to right. This shift signals a transition into the narrative proper, as we enter Jeff's parents' garage, where he sits in a tent, piling cigarette butts in a hubcap ashtray and talking on a cordless phone to one of his friends. But this reversal of movement also suggests something more—that the contours of Burnfield are such that reaching the city limits only propels us back to its center, so that we spiral inward, back toward the parking lots, strip malls, and chain restaurants that account for the better part of this town and, by extension, the contemporary American landscape.

Although Linklater had suggested doing an adaptation of *subUrbia* when he first saw the play, it was not until Bogosian visited Austin in late 1995 that both began to move forward with a film for Castle Rock (*subUrbia* [screenplay] 4). A few months later, and on a hiatus from the stalled project *The Newton Boys*, shooting on the film would commence, much of it on a corner in Austin (which became "the Corner") and mostly at night. It premiered in the fall of 1996 at the New York Film Festival and would reach mainstream release in early 1997. Although the film was once available in VHS format (and still is, used), it bears the unfortunate distinction of being the only film in Linklater's oeuvre not currently available on DVD, an absence that future distributors will, one hopes, rectify.

In the title itself, both play and film make clear their interest in a subject that has been central to the American cultural imaginary for decades now. "Always as much an *idea* as a reality," Robert Beuka notes, in *SuburbiaNation*, "the landscape of American suburbia has become and remained something of a symbolic minefield, the mirror (or, perhaps better put, the picture window) through which middle-class American culture casts its uneasy reflective gaze on itself." This gaze, Beuka observes, shares not only qualities we associate with the country's utopian "dream" of itself but "that dream's inverse: the vision of a homogenized, soulless, plastic landscape of tepid conformity, an alienating 'noplace'" (4). Such a vision might seem readily apparent to any given denizen of the sprawling communities that make up the better part of our settled landscape, though, in practice, someone might just as easily be struck by how different various communities labeled *suburban* can be. This is precisely what Jon C. Teaford argues in *The American Suburb: The Basics*, when he writes, "Only the most obtuse observers could seriously claim that America's suburbs offer a look-alike landscape with one suburban community indistinguishable from the next" (218). Regardless, the equation of suburbia with a "plastic landscape of tepid conformity" continues to be a preoccupation of American culture (one need only think of the critically popular television series *Mad Men* [2007-] as a recent example), and this set of attitudes is precisely what informs *subUrbia*, with a capital *U*—drawing attention to the prefix *sub-*, existing below, or in deference to, the urban, a place evoked in the hyperbolic visions of grandeur (a celebrity's arrival) or horror (Tim's descriptions of his travels) within the imaginary of the Burnfield youth.

In outlining a brief history of these attitudes, Beuka discusses several sociological studies that appeared in the 1950s and 1960s, all of them critical of various aspects of suburban life; interestingly, among those texts is Paul Goodman's 1960 *Growing Up Absurd,* a copy of which appears in the final Super-8 sequence of *Slacker.* There, the euphoria of the people seems to exist in counterpoint to the arguments of Goodman's book—or, at the very least, as a kind of response to the condition that Goodman outlines. That condition, as Goodman describes it, is a growing sense of stifling conformity that begins at an early age. "In our society," Goodman writes, "bright lively children, with the potentiality for knowledge, noble ideals, honest effort, and some kind of worthwhile achievement, are transformed into useless and cynical bipeds, or decent young men trapped or early resigned, whether in or out of the organized system" (14). This sense of defeat arises from a country, according to Goodman, that is "simply deficient in many of the most elementary objective opportunities and worth-while goals that could make growing up possible" (among them, "man's work," "honest public speech," and "the opportunity to be useful"). "It has no Honor. It has no Community," he states in a style closer to manifesto than sociological study (12). Some thirty years later, these ideas inform Bogosian's play and Linklater's film, and while Goodman is more critical of the culture as a whole than the suburbs as such, one could say the same for both playwright and director.

If this film and play are about an "alienating 'noplace'," in Beuka's words, the center of this noplace is "the Corner," a gas station and Laundromat building where characters eat, drink, talk, fight, crack jokes, pace nervously, lie down, get up, have sex, fall in love, break up, and, in Bee-Bee's case, lose consciousness, perhaps die, during the almost twenty-four-hour period of the narrative. In many ways, the Corner is the antithesis of social spaces like the Emporium or the Moon Tower in *Dazed and Confused;* whereas the latter provide release, places where differences can be temporarily elided, even if they persist, the Corner serves only to increase the anxiety, frustration, and despair of those who gather there, whether for social reasons or economic, as with Nazeer and Pakeesa. Bogosian's play emphasizes this pressure by restricting the entire narrative to the Corner, but Linklater's adaptation takes advantage of other locales: the opening, for example, after its credit montage, moves from Jeff's parents' garage to Buff's pizza joint and to

Sooze's bedroom and living room, where her mother watches a shopping channel, before ending at the Corner. Likewise, later scenes also visit alternative locations, including the interior of Bee-Bee's house, a Chinese restaurant, the exterior of a house where Buff steals the gnome, and a field by the side of the highway, which Jeff crosses when he leaves the limo. These departures, however, actually strengthen the magnetic pull of the Corner, since characters depart only to return. Even Pony, who has "escaped" Burnfield, finds himself drawn back to the Corner. If the title sequence functions in a kind of spiral, Dantean or otherwise, the Corner is the center around which the film rotates. Such circular structure is indicated visually throughout the film, as in the Circle-A logo of the convenience store, a nod to the anarchy symbol (and a frequent visual motif in Linklater's films). When Pony's limousine first arrives, it circles the convenience store, a motion we follow as Jeff turns his head one way, and then the other, building our anticipation but also spiraling around this center. Characters, too, sometimes circle one another when they speak to each other; Buff in particular likes to create circles whether on or off his in-line skates. The narrative, as well, might be regarded as one large circle within the setting of the Corner. At the beginning, the action takes place to the immediate right of the gas station's entrance, next to the pay phone and the Dumpster; as the film proceeds, the action moves around the building—not methodically, by any means, but to various other locations in proximity to the main building, such as scenes that take place behind the building (Jeff and Bee-Bee talking), in the van (Erica and Tim, and Jeff's later investigation), in front of the bakery (Sooze's "Burger Manifesto" performance), and in the parking lot to the left of the front of the gas station (near the front of the Laundromat, which is where most of the initial return of Pony takes place). The final scenes—Tim's return and threatening Nazeer, Jeff's attempt to defuse the confrontation, and Tim's finally finding Bee-Bee on the roof—all take place on the same side of the store as the first scene. Although the narrative's progression does not follow a perfect rotation by any means, the general movement and return of events, while being pulled always to the same basic center (the Corner itself), suggest a circular pattern, as does the imperfect, almost-twenty-four-hour period of plot time, day becoming night becoming day. Movement only brings characters back to where they began, with no accompanying sense of progression or, at the very least, joy. Even Tim, having committed murder (or so we believe), comes back to the Corner with almost no time having elapsed at all, suggesting that every action—even homicide—is without consequence or the possibility for change. If any character suggests that possibility, it is Jeff, who declares late into the film that he has reached some kind of epiphany, but in one of the great sleights-of-hand in the original play, he is never allowed to deliver it, instead becoming a bystander to the implosion of his relationship with Sooze and the seeming realization of Tim's perverse predictions.

If Beuka's "noplace" description aptly describes the film's attitude toward the suburbs, then this circularity without progression suggests a sense of "notime" as well. Burnfield embodies a present temporality that does not encourage a kind of Thoreau-inspired, reflective response, an attendance to which might leave open the possibility for intellectual growth, but instead a state of futility in which present actions accrue without meaning, though dire consequences are suffered just the same. And accompanying this present-ness without progression is a sense of the past as malleable, beholden to no stable sense of history. Consider, for example, the delicate series of exchanges between Jeff and Pony when Pony has just arrived. Buff notes that Jeff *and* Pony started the band, which Jeff confirms, but in a self-deprecating way—"Well, I helped start it, but, you know, uh . . ." Instead of reading Jeff's cue, however, as a sign to agree with him, Pony responds with, "Well, uh, not exactly," setting off a brief dispute over Jeff's involvement in the band's early days (largely filtered through uncomfortable, phony laughter). Pony, for example, says that they "jammed a couple of times" but that this occurred "before we were really a band"; Jeff, however, replies, "Yeah, well, I, I came by more than a couple of times." Before any consensus is reached, Tim arrives, and the conversation shifts. Both Giovanni Ribisi (Jeff) and Jayce Bartok (Pony) play the scene well, with Ribisi burying his argument in his characteristic slur and Bartok burying his within a slightly forced, not-so-easygoing laughter. And while the dialogue I have cited here comes from the film, neither play nor film ever presents a more "true" version of that history. To be sure, the viewer is likely to side with Jeff, given how sympathetic he is in comparison to Pony. Nonetheless, one can see that Jeff has just as many motives to imagine himself a greater part of a now successful band as Pony has to imagine Jeff as having had almost nothing to do with his success. The past provides no solace for Jeff—nor does it seem to ease Pony, either. Later, in a related moment, a far darker imagining of the very immediate past occurs when Tim tells Jeff that he has killed Erica, allowing Jeff to believe this false event until Erica appears in the limousine to pick up Buff the next morning. In this case, the audience eventually is given a true version of events—that is, Erica is still alive. But the point has been made. Jeff, the protagonist of a noplace, notime setting, exists in a postmodern state unmoored from the present, so that his best intentions to affect the world are thwarted by his inability to leave a life he is partly culpable in having created. Rather than provide a potential for creativity or release, the Corner's temporality, both progressionless present and malleable past, tends to encourage the very worst in destructive behavior, such as the verbal abuse the Corner kids direct toward Nazeer and Pakeesa, a general xenophobia that afflicts all characters, even Jeff; Tim's brandishing of his gun (we never see whether he might actually use it); and the self-directed violence of Bee-Bee's suicide, the consequences of which end both play and film, though the film's ambiguity over Bee-Bee's condition mitigates this a bit more than the play, where Jeff's clearly stating "She's dead" forecloses any sense of release or, for that matter, hope (121).

None of this is to say, however, that *subUrbia* avoids the creative act, a subject in so many of Linklater's films. Unlike *Slacker,* however, which finds humor in the activities of its Austin residents, even as it asks the viewer to treat the characters with respect, *subUrbia* has a more satiric view, mostly with regard to Pony. His name, of course, recalls many clichés: "one-trick pony," "dog-and-pony show," and even "one-horse town" (directed less at Pony than Burnfield). The film constantly underscores Pony's superficiality; it is no coincidence that he speaks lovingly of his life in Los Angeles, traditionally a bête noire for New York artists such as Bogosian or those, like Linklater, from Austin. In relation to that life, he recalls star sightings—Sandra Bernhard and Johnny Depp—to indicate how well he is doing, his own celebrity growing by proximity to theirs. Of course, Pony, too, is a celebrity, the glossy sheen associated with the corporate rock star carefully constructed to appear unrehearsed and casual, an attitude nowhere more apparent than when he sings "Man Invisible" for the group in the parking lot of the Circle A. "Unplugged Pony," Buff calls it, in reference to the television series *MTV Unplugged* (1989–), a program that relies upon a gap between audience and performer that the show promises to close, through intimate settings, low lighting, and mostly acoustic instruments, even though such intimacy often paradoxically increases distance (as it does, for example, with Hollywood stars, in the long history of fan publications and personal profiles that go back to the studios' earliest days). Likewise, Pony's proximity has a similar effect: the more he hangs around, the more mirage-like the promise of escape associated with his presence begins to seem. Emphasizing this even further are the lyrics of "Man Invisible," which detail a suburban nightmare, a family killed in a minivan accident, one that might have stopped for snacks here at the Circle A before setting out on the open road. The message is, if you leave the Corner, you die. Even if one finds some brief aural respite within the film's soundtrack itself—scored by Sonic Youth, a band that would seem to operate counter to Pony in almost every way—we are left, in the end, on the Corner once again, this time with Tim, Jeff, and Nazeer, as we wait for Bee-Bee's ambulance, an odd, ironic fulfillment of the fatal consequences of "Man Invisible."

To return to the circular pattern, might we then say that there really is a kind of Dantean descent here—that in order to leave Burnfield, we have to go through the roughly twenty-four-hour period on the Corner? Can we imagine Jeff's leaving? Can we imagine that Sooze and Buff have futures beyond the thin promises made by Pony's manager and Pony himself? The film is ultimately ambivalent on these questions. We have, at the end, a montage similar to the beginning, and the film (in true circle form) ends with the shot with which it begins, the sign that beckons, "Welcome to Burnfield." On the one hand, this might be the final image one would see upon leaving the town—in one's rearview mirror. On the other hand, the repetition of this sign might also indicate a return—that we are being once again drawn into the Corner, into another twenty-four-hour period that, however different the circumstances, will feel the same. Or, even more disturbingly, perhaps we will experience *the same twenty-four-hour period,* as though we are doomed to relive the lives of Jeff, Sooze, Pony, Tim, Buff, Nazeer, Pakeesa, Erica, and Bee-Bee, on this same night, over and over again, ad infinitum. However we read this final image, a much darker, much less hopeful vision of a present temporality pervades this film, one that later films directed by

Linklater will take up as well—though his next film, *The Newton Boys,* will be considerably lighter.

The Newton Boys was an important film for Linklater's early career, as much for its failures critically and financially as for the risks it took. Its budget, twenty-seven million dollars, was significantly higher than anything he had directed before; its plot covered a five-year time span, as opposed to the mostly twenty-four-hour periods of previous films, save *It's Impossible;* and the production design was more elaborate than *Dazed's* own period-specific details. Originally begun as the second of a two-picture deal with Castle Rock (the first being *Before Sunrise*), in 1995 the film would move to Fox, with whom Linklater and Detour Filmproduction would face regular conflicts until the film's eventual release in March 1998, when it opened to low box office and poor reviews, despite a notable exception in Jonathan Rosenbaum's *Chicago Reader* column as well as a spot in the critic's top-ten list of that year. The lackluster critical reception and low financial returns contributed to the period that followed, where Linklater began projects only to see them fall through, including adaptations of the books *Rivethead* and *Friday Night Lights,* prior to his making *Waking Life.* Yet when one actually revisits the film from a contemporary perspective, the pleasures it affords are many, and its light tone belies the difficulties in its making and the problems that followed. (Alison Macor's chapter on the film's production history, "Winning the Battle, Losing the War," in her *Chainsaws, Slackers, and Spy Kids,* is an excellent, detailed resource on the multiple issues the film faced [188–220].)

A January 1994 *Smithsonian* article sparked Detour's initial interest. In "Every Time a Bank Was Robbed, They Thought It Was Us," Claude Stanush, a "former *Life* correspondent and newspaper columnist," narrates the true story of four brothers, the Newtons, and their gang, who robbed "60 banks, 6 trains" in the early 1920s before being caught in one of the largest heists of its day, the Rondout, Illinois, robbery of June 12, 1924. History, according to Stanush, had forgotten the brothers, an absence he had attempted to rectify, meeting both Willis and Joe Newton as early as 1973 and coproducing a 1976 documentary with David Middleton, *The Newton Boys: Portrait of an Outlaw Gang* (both Stanush and Middleton would also later release a book by the same name, with Willis and Joe credited as authors and Stanush and Middleton serving "as told to" roles) (Newton et al. xvi). Stanush would follow his interest in the brothers to the film itself, contributing to its screenplay, also authored by Clark Walker, Linklater, and, late in the process, John Sayles. No doubt because of Stanush's background as a journalist rather than a historian, the original *Smithsonian* piece includes details typical historiography might leave out, such as Willis's relating an anecdote "with a grin" or longer passages describing the brothers during a visit to Stanush's home: "One day Joe suddenly dropped to the ground to skylight a bee that had just risen, straight up like a helicopter, from a wildflower. By silhouetting it against the sky, Joe could tell the location of its hive as it made a beeline for home." The article's tendency to rely heavily on the brothers' own testimony, combined with Stanush's personal memories of Willis and Joe, reads as both tall tale and historical fact, a blend in keeping with one of the primary genres the film draws upon, the western.

Although much of the publicity of the film seemed to present a gangster film—poster images of the four brothers in period suits, hair slicked back, carrying guns, one aimed at the camera—the film is also very much a western, from the outset, where, after a credit sequence presented in the style of much older films (including sepia tone, intertitle borders, old-style character introductions, and even a caption under the title reading "Passed By The National Board of Review"), an iris-out opens onto a full-color long shot of a man walking down a country road. This is Willis, we learn, returning from prison, who finds Jess and Joe breaking a horse. The landscape (wide-open country), the costumes (cowboy hats), the narrative itself (breaking horses), and even the score (banjo and fiddle that pick up in tempo when Joe's horse begins to buck) are familiar conventions of the western, like many that appear throughout the film. Underscoring this connection even further is the film's self-conscious acknowledgment of westerns in a scene where Willis, Louise, and Lewis emerge from a movie theater and Willis and Lewis debate the relative merits of early western stars William S. Hart and Tom Mix. After this brief exchange, both Willis and Lewis race down the stairs in pursuit of a chocolate malt, knocking each other out of the way in some entertaining physical comedy that emphasizes Willis's boyishness. The juxtaposition of the early western references with Willis's clowning around draws on associations of the genre as light, fun, and appealing to a young spectator; such qualities are evident elsewhere in the film, in interactions among the brothers, as in the scene immediately preceding this one, where they wrestle one another upon Doc's arrival, a nod to the physical humor in many westerns. Other allusions inflect the film, such as a comically large explosion in the third bank robbery that recalls Butch's underestimation of dynamite's power in *Butch Cassidy and the Sundance Kid*, or a shot of Jess's firing almost directly into the camera following Willis and Louis's race for ice cream, a reference to the famous final shot (or first, depending upon the exhibitor) of *The Great Train Robbery* (1903). The film draws on other genres as well—the heist film, the gangster film—and is indebted not only to the western but to the history of cinema itself. In even more self-conscious references to the latter, for example, the brothers are jailed early in their exploits for a crime they did not commit, the robbery of a "picture show," and the explosive liquid used to blow the safes, nitroglycerin, sounds much like the flammable chemical used in early film stock, nitrate, an unintentional connection that nonetheless presents itself in a film so aware of and indebted to the medium's past.

But Stanush's original article was not a western; it reached for empirical fact and identified itself as history, even as it slid into a more romantic view of the brothers and painted them in mythic proportions, heroes of a sort, an image difficult to avoid given the incredible events Willis and Joe narrate and the ways, more broadly, in which the American West has itself been conceptualized. Writing in 1931, only seven years after the brothers' incarceration, Walter Prescott Webb attempted to debunk a more romantic view of the West that even then held sway; for Webb, such views originated in the East: "The East set the standards, wrote the books, and made the laws. What it did not comprehend was strange, romantic, spectacular" (495). (Stanush called Webb's *Great Plains*, from which this passage is taken, a "classic book" in a letter to the *Smithsonian* published three years before his article on the Newtons, a reference that suggests an even more direct influence than is discussed here ["Barbed Wire"].) Of course, like many attempts to demystify (including, quite often, those aimed at cinema itself), Webb's book reinforced the West as separate, distinct from other regions, and, in spite of itself, romantic. Historiographies of the West, whether professional or amateur, argumentative or anecdotal, old or new, have perhaps always been vulnerable to these tendencies, as much as the fictional narratives against which they sometimes set themselves as correcting. In their darker moments, both can elide suffering, such as the treatment of Native Americans, referenced only briefly in *The Newton Boys* when a Native American saloon owner buys a drink for Willis, Glasscock, and Slim. Yet just as they distort, both can illuminate—whether despite or because of such romanticism. Juxtaposing two versions of western history that appeared in 1893—one, Colonel William F. Cody's theatrical performance "Buffalo Bill's Wild West and Congress of Rough Riders of the World," and the other, Frederick Jackson Turner's essay "The Significance of the Frontier in American History"—Rick Worland and Edward Countryman reflect, "It is not enough to fall back on an easy distinction between 'myth' (Cody) and 'history' (Turner). Cody and Turner both had stories to tell. Each story had and still has its truth" (184). Given this own volume's interest in temporality, such ideas inform the way this film, in its drawing on history (both that of the Newtons and that of cinema itself) as well as myth (particularly in its generic connections), reveals its own truths about the events it depicts, the cinematic experience, and the idea of present temporalities. *The Newton Boys'* interest in history, in fact, lies in a desire to represent events with some degree of accuracy while also exploring the more mythic characters of its outlaw cowboy-thieves that Stanush originally described; in addition—and more important for this book, given its focus—*The Newton Boys* seeks to open up those events to the present in which they were lived and to allow viewers to experience, if only briefly, the past as a lived present in which outcomes were not known and consequences had not been met. Although this idea itself is hardly revelatory, the film's exploration of it is deft and, quite often, fascinating.

One early, small moment that illustrates the film's interest in the experience of the present occurs during the first bank robbery. Although Willis committed earlier robberies in his life, this is the first robbery of the film, set up as the one where Willis, a quick study, will learn what to do by negative example, basing the brothers' future success partly on the missteps made here. The sequence begins in classic western fashion—three men, on horseback, arrive in town and receive suspicious looks from men sitting across the street. After dismounting, two of them, Willis and Slim, enter the bank, and once inside, Willis approaches the teller. Instead of announcing his intentions immediately, however, he exchanges a "Howdy" with the teller and simply stands there, looking askance, smiling to himself at a private joke (figure 5). He even begins laughing a bit, as the teller, too, joins him. These actions create a sense of delay, as the cuts slow slightly (one shot, from the teller's side of the desk, lingers longer than others) and the score momentarily ceases. Like the moment in *Before Sunrise* when Celine delays stepping off the train, Willis's delay is ours as well, since until he pulls his gun, we too must wait. In fact, the whole scene is predicated on a subdued approach to narrative. When Willis eventually does pull his gun, the bank does not erupt into action, but instead, another customer, an old man, slowly looks up from the counter, before the film cuts to outside of the bank, where another old man approaches the bank slowly, to be led inside at gunpoint by Glasscock, on lookout. The men then trot away on horseback at a leisurely pace before a car catches up with them, at which point the forward momentum of the film picks up again. But the robbery itself, particularly when Willis expresses his own personal amusement, draws our attention to a moment preceding action, where very little seems to occur. This suggests a self-awareness on the film's part not only about narrative and genre—through such delays, *The Newton Boys* reminds us of the powerful ways in which both shape our expectations in any given moment—but about history as well. Willis, the actual Willis, could not predict what might happen after one of his robberies, and he certainly

Figure 5. Narrative delay in *The Newton Boys*: Willis's bemusement at the first robbery.

would have had no idea of the Rondout robbery in the days of his early heists, much less the sense that he would serve time, later be free, and eventually be the subject of a magazine article, a book, a documentary, and a feature film (the term *documentary* would not have even been in currency, in relation to film, when his first robberies were committed). Historical films often remind us of moments preceding an inevitable event, but in doing so, they frequently encourage a sense of fatalism. The love story of *From Here to Eternity* (1953) seems doomed from the outset, since viewers anticipate the Japanese bombing of Pearl Harbor well before it occurs within the film. *The Newton Boys* is not immune from such fatalism, dropping hints that the Rondout job will be dangerous and should not be undertaken. Yet, despite gestures in that direction, the film often offers a sense of possibility in the present, as here, when Willis delays pulling his gun and reminds us of the illusion of historical inevitability. Although it is hardly radical in its destabilizing fixed notions of history, it does encourage a sense of agency in the experience of the present, as much for historical figures who had no sense of a particular event's later consequences as for an audience member's own time. Jonathan Rosenbaum, discussing his fascination for the scene when two characters watch the film *Greed* (1924) after a robbery, describes it as "a mysterious parenthesis . . . a discreet pocket of bliss in which audience members are invited to lose themselves," a description that might fit this scene's own subtle experiments with narrative delay, ones the film explores elsewhere as well. As Rosenbaum notes in relation to his own list of such examples, "These moments . . . invariably stop the storytelling dead in its tracks, inviting viewers to climb inside the space and roam around."

In terms of its narrative, however, the film is actually more structured than this discussion of delays, pauses, and "parenthes[es]" might suggest (or it may be that delay requires a more steady, insistent pace to be effective). Six main heists guide the plot (five in the first half of the film): the first, Willis's initiation, ultimately a success; the second, Willis's learning about nitrate from Glasscock, and Jess and Joe's initiation, also successful; the third, Doc's initiation, again a success; the fourth, a failure, a rounded safe that resists nitrate; the fifth, a second failure, a sloppily executed theft while in Canada; and the sixth, the Rondout debacle, which constitutes most of the second half and ends with Doc critically wounded and the brothers eventually incarcerated. Within that more general Aristotelian rise and fall, however, the film, in its fascination with the idiosyncratic details of the robberies it depicts and the lives of the brothers before and after robberies (particularly Willis), often explores a present temporality, small delays and pauses that seem to forestall the inevitable structuring and restructuring of the heists, of plot as well as memory, myth as well as history, even if as spectators we are still carried along in the narrative drift. Long, leisurely scenes take place between the robberies themselves—most of the film, in fact, is composed of what the brothers do when they are *not* robbing banks—and even within the robberies, inaction supplements action, leading to the sense that the heists, while exciting and dangerous, often just as much involved their fair share of waiting. Consider, for example, the second robbery, where, after a long shot of Jess crossing the street in the dark, a medium shot captures Jess and Joe talking to one another outside of the bank; at the end of the shot, the two brothers laugh, humor underscoring the absurdity of the situation for the brothers but also for us, for whom the idea of bank heists is for the most part, thankfully, far removed. Both brothers, new to this, have no idea what to expect, and this creates a sense of the present as possibility, potential energy not yet become kinetic (or the inherent kineticism of waiting itself). Much of the third robbery takes place outside of the banks, in the interactions of the brothers (cutting the phone line, joking with the security guard, Jess making fun of Joe) and in long shots of a darkened main street, snow sweeping across as the wind blows, that indicate a larger fascination for the western's quieter, atmospheric moments. While the scene certainly provides dramatic action—Doc's "two-step" method of breaking into the banks (first, the shotgun; second, the shoulder in the door), the unanticipated approach of the farmer making his way through town (a historical detail from Stanush's original article), the enormous explosion that takes place on both ends of the street—it also is often just as interested in the dynamics of the brothers when they are simply waiting, as when Jess teases Joe for his mishandling of the farmer's driving through town, which is also the end of the scene, thus skipping the literal and figurative payoff of the money itself. Also connected to a sense of present-ness in the film's temporality is Willis's enthusiasm for improvisation, whether in his proposing they rob not one but two banks after cutting the phone lines in the third robbery or in his inventing the plan for the fifth robbery in the immediate aftermath of the failed fourth—and, even, changing it *again* right before it happens. To be sure, *The Newton Boys* is far from avant-garde in its exploration of temporality. It has none of the formal experiments of *It's Impossible,* and its overall narrative structure is fairly standard. Nonetheless, the film's brief digressions and drifting narrative, however modest, resist the seeming inevitability of time in both narrative and historiography.

A present temporality informs the next three films directed by Linklater, although they are not, technically speaking, films. Though very different in style and subject matter, all three make use of the same basic format: the digital.

Dreaming in Digital, Motel Confessions, and the Poet of Wall Street

Late within *Waking Life,* the protagonist, having emerged yet again from one dream only to find himself in another, performs what many of us do in our minds, while asleep: a mundane task, rather than something fantastical. For this protagonist, that activity is watching television, and while channel surfing, he comes across Steven Soderbergh telling a story about Louis Malle and Billy Wilder. Malle has recently completed an expensive picture, one priced at $2.5 million. When Wilder asks after its subject, Malle says, "Well, it's sort of a dream within a dream"; Soderbergh deadpans Wilder's reply: "You've just lost two-and-a-half-million dollars." While the budgetary story here recalls the financial problems of *The Newton Boys,* even as it humorously acknowledges the potential for this one, too, to see very little in the way of profits, the anecdote equally recognizes the film's own spirited eclecticism, one that will carry into the next two features as well: the claustrophobic, slowly building theater adaptation *Tape* and the brief, meandering short tour of New York City, courtesy Timothy "Speed" Levitch, *Live from Shiva's Dance Floor.* But *Waking Life,* more than the two that follow and perhaps more than any other in Linklater's oeuvre to date, announces itself from the outset as something quite different. Partly, that difference registers in its choice of medium, digital video, a format Linklater had never used before but one he would revisit in both *Tape* and *Shiva.* Unlike those films, however,

Waking Life underwent an unusual, extensive postproduction process, one that altered its images significantly, so that its most striking aspect is also its most obvious: an animation style called digital rotoscoping. Digital rotoscoping derives from an older technique known simply as rotoscoping, where an artist draws over already existing film footage in order to create realistic movement and shape within the animation. For *Waking Life,* Bob Sabiston, working with Tommy Pallotta (who appears in Slacker as "Looking for Missing Friend"), digitized the process, using a computer to "interpolate" moments between lines of the artist's own creation. (Sabiston and Pallotta had previously put digital rotoscoping to use on shorter works such as *Snack and Drink* [1999].) The result is an uncanny blend of cartoon and document, a visual style that takes advantage of older technologies and new ones, as indicated in the stylus Sabiston's team members used in order to mark the screen. Watching an animator work, computerized "pen" in hand, one cannot help but recall Alexandre Astruc's famous 1948 call for a new cinema, "The birth of a new avant-garde: La caméra-stylo," in which the French writer and filmmaker saw new horizons opening for the cinema, so that nearly any text or subject matter, through the filmmaker's "camera-pen," would be possible: "a form in which and by which an artist can express his thoughts, however abstract they may be, or translate his obsessions exactly as he does in the contemporary essay or novel" (18). (I take my cue here from those who have seen in new technologies the further elaborations of Astruc's vision—figures such as Jean-Pierre Geuens, who has discussed, for example, small digital equipment that allows for a filmmaker to "[think] on the spot and 'writ[e]' with his or her camera" [24].) Although digital rotoscoping is not exactly what Astruc had in mind, the accidental conjunction of *caméra-stylo* and computer-pen nonetheless reveals ways in which Linklater's film is, in fact, closer to Astruc's ideals than might at first appear. Much like Astruc's vision, the film pulls in many diverse areas of human inquiry; Linklater has referred to the film as a "kitchen-sink movie," filled to the brim with questions such as, "Who are we? What are we made up of? And is it ours? Is it everybody's? What do we share? How are we separate? How are we together?" ("Commentary by the Filmmakers"). Additionally, the film is a memory palace of Linklater's films to date, with characters reappearing from past films both directly, as Celine and Jesse from *Before Sunrise* do, and indirectly, as with the actors who played them. (I like to imagine that Mike and Clint from *Dazed*, Adam Goldberg and Nicky Katt, have buried the hatchet later in life over a mutual affection for Debord.)

Arriving in 2001, and using its medium so innovatively, *Waking Life* seemed both to crystallize and to debunk an attitude that, in the face of aging celluloid archives, new distribution networks, alternative exhibition contexts, general millennial anxieties, and, most important, the rise of the digital, was for many assured: that we had witnessed the end of cinema. Recognizing cinema's last days has become a common academic preoccupation, especially with regard to the advent and proliferation of digital technologies, often characterized as undermining something fundamental in the image's relationship with reality. "What concerns me," wrote Dai Vaughan in the winter of 1994–1995, "is that we shall wake up one day and find that the assumption of a privileged relationship between a photograph and its object, an assumption which has held good for 150 years and on which ciné-actuality is founded, will have ceased to be operative" (188). For Vaughan, this privileged relationship was bound to change because of the fundamentally different ways that digital cinema collected and stored data; Vaughan and many others fear that the unspoken contract of photography and film, one hinging on the relative truth value of the referent, is broken with the all too easily manipulated digital. *Waking Life* would in a sense seem to confirm this apocalyptic reading, given its whimsical, uninhibited approach to digital manipulation. But we might read it as responding to these debates in other ways. Both Steven Shaviro and Markos Hadjioannou have shown how *Waking Life* either expresses older ideas about film (Shaviro) or ideas about the digital that, while distinct from analog, do not prefigure cinema's death (Hadjioannou). In fact, Hadjioannou's interests in creativity and active engagement are very close to this book's approach, but whereas both Shaviro and Hadjioannou address important medium-specific questions, my own sense is that the film, even as it conjures these inquiries, sidesteps them, too, by exploring other aspects of the cinematic experience—and, in so doing, defining that experience beyond the digital-analog dichotomy, in ways that also tie into the primary focus of this book.

One way *Waking Life* engages with ideas about cinema is through its on-screen depiction of filmgoing. On two separate occasions, the protagonist goes to a movie: *Noise & Silence*, an avant-garde silent short, narrated by a very well-spoken chimpanzee, and "The Holy Moment," a documentary or narrative conversation between two friends (although the title designates the scene as a whole rather than the film exclusively). The first takes place in a classroom, while the second is set in an opulent theater evoking the heyday of the classical era. Seeing the protagonist absorb image and sound in both exhibition spaces reminds us how active the cinema experience is in practice, despite its frequent characterization as a passive one. In *Noise & Silence*, protagonist and audience must construct connections between the lecturer's poetic monologue and the images that unfold on-screen (a man running downhill, a live music show, and others), such active engagement underscored all the more by the classroom setting (a joke as well about places where people sometimes fall asleep). "The Holy Moment" also demonstrates the active nature of spectatorship; although the protagonist is seated, silently absorbing the scene, we can see the screen reflected in his eyes, completing the circuit, as it were. And of course, on another level, the protagonist's unconscious is creating each film at the moment of projection, so that he is both author and viewer at the same time (an aspect of dreaming that Linklater has discussed). All of this hews closely to Dudley Andrew's observation that, while on the screen "a world . . . unfolds according to the design of its emplotment" at the same time "the viewer projects himself or herself toward the screen, taking the film beyond its original context into frameworks unforeseen by its maker" (91). That is, as much as the film is projected, the protagonist, too, projects, just as we do, wherever we are when we see it, which might include, beyond the classroom and theater represented here, a television, a computer, a cell phone, or any number of other possible screens that characterize life in the twenty-first century.

Of course, one could argue that any perception, whether of a film, a memory, a dream, or reality itself, requires an active process of meaning making. One would be right. But given *Waking Life*'s central preoccupations, this idea is particularly well articulated here in relation to cinema, and it manifests itself not only in these direct depictions of seeing a film but in more indirect ways as well. For example, the plot, like that in *It's Impossible* or *Slacker*, is so vague and thin that it self-consciously acknowledges a desire for narrative coherence that we associate with more traditional cinemas, even as such coherence is gently refused. While the ending seems to provide closure, bringing us full circle to the opening image of a figure floating skyward, we still have no way of knowing the protagonist's state throughout the film, whether dreaming, dead, or both. Likewise, who is the boy at the beginning, playing with a little girl before ascending, his reach for a car-door handle failing to keep him grounded? Is he the protagonist himself as a boy, an invented character, a personification of his own youthful spirit, or some combination, in the ways that dreams are quite comfortable with their own internal contradictions? The film never answers; viewers must complete these narratives on their own (or at least make the choice not to complete them). Likewise, a similar process of completion occurs with the animation, which provides detail but withholds a great deal, too, within varying degrees of specificity and abstraction. Consider, for example, the scene between two women in a coffee shop, played by Carol Dawson and Lisa Moore, when they are discussing the ways that they once imagined their current ages and how different the actual experiences are from their previous conceptions (figure 6). The animation here emphasizes facial features, hair, and clothing with lines and color but does not fill in every detail, such as Dawson's hair, its texture suggested with a few wavy strands, or Moore's shirt, its collar shaded on one side but

Figure 6. Animation style in *Waking Life*:
Moore discusses identity.

indicated only by a barely visible line on the other. Watching the film, we complete these images. And while this occurs throughout *Waking Life*, Moore makes this concept even more evident in her discussion of Benedict Anderson, as she riffs on his ideas about identity construction to surmise that a photograph of oneself in infancy becomes an occasion for narrative, as we must imagine the link between our adult self and that much younger one. "So," as she concludes, "it takes a story that's actually a fiction to make you and the baby in the picture identical—to create your identity." The adult projects this fiction onto the picture, just as viewers project onto the film, itself a projection.

The sense of an active meaning-making process in the cinemagoing experience is, in this film, tied to musings on the experience of time, whether waking or sleeping. In fact, nowhere else in Linklater's body of work, with the exception of the *Before* films, does one find so much explicit discussion of time, and one sees a recurring investment in the instant and the moment. One early figure observes, "To say yes to one instant is to say yes to all of existence"; the very next speaker, speculating that "we are in a very significant moment in history," reflects, "The moment is not just a passing, empty nothing, yet . . . it's empty with such fullness, that the great moment, the great life of the universe, is pulsating in it." Another figure discusses the "flawed perfection" that is "sufficient and complete in every single, ineffable moment," and Speed Levitch, making an early appearance here, discusses the "ongoing wow" that "is happening right now." These perspectives suggest the importance of being attuned to the present moment, even if such attention is impossible to sustain, and that attending to one moment might lead to greater insights that extend beyond it. They also suggest how mysterious and rich temporality is, when considered in itself, and in this way, they echo multiple philosophers, theologians, and thinkers who have also attempted to articulate the experience of time (as in the passages from Thoreau that open this volume). Other temporal interests within the film hinge not so much on the present as on time's fluidity, such as the difference between dream and waking time that informs Celine and Jesse's discussion, along with a subjective desire for time to slow down, as in their previous film, though here the lovers do not want to delay the inevitable train departure so much as the inevitable need to leave the bed. And whether discussing these aspects of time or experiencing his own gradual awakenings, the protagonist relies on other people to enable both. Late in the film, a woman makes this connection explicit when she tells the protagonist, "I want real human moments. I want to see you. I want you to see me." Self-awareness requires an engagement with other people in order to be effective. But for this protagonist, other people *are* himself, since he projects them, though those projections are influenced very much by his memories of past encounters with people, books, films, and other experiences that stimulated his imagination from without. A sense of circulation and movement thus characterizes these encounters between himself and others, as it does the ways that characters discuss the instant and the moment, the process of completion occasioned by narrative and animation, and the active meaning making more generally represented by the on-screen attendance of screenings and the off-screen reception of viewers.

In addition, movement is inscribed in the images themselves; faces, bodies, objects, and locales constantly pulse and shift, within and against one another. Lest this kineticism be too distracting, a dialectic emerges early between image and sound, so that the variations in the former are sutured by consistent music, voice, and ambient sound, such as the quasi-documentary noises of shoes dropping on the floor and the rustle of fabric as the protagonist gets into bed during one early scene. In this way, the film provides a sense of coherence even as it also calls for viewers to linger on the details of individual scenes and styles; more than most films, *Waking Life*, in the diverse styles of its animators, inscribes traces of its collective auteurism quite directly into its mise-en-scène. In addition, the constant shifting within the image, no matter the artist, reminds us that cinema is movement. Tom Gunning has recently made this idea central to his reflections on film; at one point, drawing on an early piece of writing by Christian Metz, Gunning describes how Metz saw on-screen movement not as "a 'picture' of motion, but instead as an experience of seeing something truly moving." Gunning explains: "In terms of a visual experience of motion, therefore, no difference exists between watching a film of a ball rolling down a hill, say, and seeing an actual ball rolling down a hill" (43). Although Gunning explains how this "invokes possibility and a future" (42), movement is equally of the present—quoting Metz, it creates "a sense of 'There it is'" (41), or, as Gunning himself describes it, "a sense of perceptual richness or immediate involvement in the image" (42). As a result, Gunning notes that movement is participatory: "Cinema, the projected moving image, demands that we participate in the movement we perceive" (42). *Waking Life* emphasizes this aspect of cinematic experience through an unusual animation style, its constant movement emphasizing the present moment and the cinema as an active, participatory process—for a man who may or may not be dead as he wanders through a dreamworld, for a boy who may or may not be him, for the characters that both encounter, and for viewers, especially, as we wake from the dream of the film into that of our own lives.

While *Waking Life* keeps us off-balance, unable to right ourselves within continually mutating, multiple settings, Linklater's next film, *Tape,* occupies the real-time, single space of a motel room in Lansing, Michigan, in the early evening hours. Here, a forced reunion takes place among three high school friends—Vince, Jon, and Amy—as they revisit what happened at the end of their senior year, when a sexual encounter between Jon and Amy became violent, Vince's alleging, and Jon's confirming, that Jon raped her, with Amy both agreeing with and complicating that assessment all at once. For this film, funding came from a relatively new production company, InDigEnt, formed by director Gary Winick, Alexis Alexanian, and John Sloss (producer on several of Linklater's films), in conjunction with the Independent Film Channel, in 1999. Conceived by Winick after seeing Thomas Vinterberg's film *The Celebration* (1998), InDigEnt was designed, aesthetically, to encourage the use of digital video and, economically, to keep costs low (Winick would also direct one of the company's films, *Tadpole* [2002]) (Restuccio). This production arrangement suited *Tape* well, a close adaptation of Stephen Belber's one-act play, which Uma Thurman and Ethan Hawke, who portray Amy and Vince, had sent Linklater in hopes that the project would interest the director. Filling out the three-character cast was Robert Sean Leonard, adding an often-cited perverse but effective intertextual layer to the film, one referencing Hawke's and Leonard's roles as prep-school roommates in *Dead Poets Society* (1989). Rehearsing for a few weeks in a motel room in New Jersey and even, late in the process, on the set itself, a soundstage in Manhattan, Linklater and company would shoot the low-budget film over the course of six days, with cinematography provided by Maryse Alberti and Linklater on "two consumer-model Sony PAL digital cameras" ("Commentary with Richard Linklater & Ethan Hawke"). Such cameras allowed for a dynamism not out of keeping with *Waking Life*, although in this case, the movement comes not from the combination of animator whimsy and computer interpolation but the cameras' handheld fluidity in conjunction with clever editing. *Tape* premiered at the Sundance Film Festival in 2001, three days after *Waking Life*.

At the center of this film is the trauma of a past event, the effects of that trauma on all three characters, and the truth of what really occurred, which is both self-evident and elusive. On the one hand, Jon's recorded admission of rape, coming as it does as a response to the pressure of Vince's questions, would seem to confirm what happened, as would other scenes, none more so than Amy's description of what she hopes will happen to Jon when he dies ("My hope is that your last living sensation be that of a steel rod being shoved repeatedly up your insides"). But other aspects of *Tape* make the memories of events more uncertain. For one, Amy herself, when asked by Vince whether Jon raped her, denies it, and later, after delivering the line about Jon's last stages of death, turns her head, smiles, and asks, "Is that along the lines of what you wanted?"—calling out both men for their stake in "helping" her. In his review for the *New York Times*, Stephen Holden compares the murkiness of the conflicting accounts to Akira Kurosawa's famous film dealing with similar concerns: "And as the questions fly, the story becomes a "Rashomon"-like exploration of the past, which each person remembers differently." Although Lynn Turner, in her sharply rendered "Wind Up" for the academic journal *Camera Obscura*, counters that the film is "no *Rashomon*" (115), she, too, notes several queries left unanswered ("What could or what should we deduce from the evidence provided? What happened?" [128]), exploring Amy's use of irony in her dealings with Vince and Jon. In any case, the idea that truth itself is inherently mercurial, impossible to ascertain with any degree of clarity, resonates highly with contemporary ideas about the difficulties of establishing veracity in our post-Newtonian, media-saturated lives. Add to that the fact that this film's truth hinges on a trauma of the past, and we must ask, to what extent can any truth be clarified in the present, much less one of past trauma being brought to bear on the present?

Such questions take on particular urgency within cinema, where debates about representing the past have played out historically within the work of writers articulating the mysterious power of the screen, whether to demystify or dwell in it. Confronted with these ideas, we may find ourselves drawn to philosophies of postmodernism in which any notion of truth is suspect. This idea is precisely what critic Linda Williams explores within her essay "Mirrors without Memories: Truth, History, and *The Thin Blue Line.*" Working off Oliver Wendell Holmes's description of a photograph as a "mirror with a memory" (379), she describes what cinema has lost in relation to a sense of reliability and truth: "What was once a 'mirror with a memory' can now only reflect another mirror" (380). Although Williams is writing about documentary, where concerns of truth and representation are often more urgent than narrative films, her descriptions fit very much with *Tape,* particularly since she, too, writes about works that investigate the traumas of the past: Errol Morris's *Thin Blue Line* (1988), about a murder, and Claude Lanzmann's *Shoah* (1985), about the Holocaust. But rather than suggest that an attempt to represent the truth "inevitably succumbs to a depthlessness of the simulacrum" or that truth is abandoned within the "undecidabilities of representation," she instead attempts to carve out an alternative space for postmodern understandings of truth by saying that "there can be historical depth to the notion of truth—not the depth of unearthing a coherent and unitary past, but the depth of the past's reverberation with the present." Drawing on the two primary films she discusses, she concludes, "Our best response to this crisis of representation might be to do what Lanzmann and Morris do: to deploy the many facets of these mirrors to reveal the seduction of lies" (394). We might consider *Tape* as doing the same: that is, although it cannot provide a final truth of events, it can "reveal the seduction of lies" that have elided them, through the mirror of its medium. Thus, unlike the loss of history we generally associate with postmodernism, *Tape* enables an attendance to the present that does not jettison the past but invites it into the space that these characters occupy, where they may, slowly, as the evening progresses, begin to experience a small sense of the pain still cast by a past trauma, even if they cannot piece together with any certainty the events themselves. *Tape* thus reaches toward an attendance to the present in which the past would inform the current moment without losing any of its inherent complexities, contradictions, or opacity, yet still allow some reflection (to use the mirror metaphor) of the original trauma in the room, to leave open the possibility for mourning.

That said, the film evinces an awareness for the difficulties inherent in representation from the outset. Belber's original play stages some bits of business for Vince, prior to Jon's arrival, ones essentially repeated in the film—drinking one beer while pouring another down the sink, throwing the empty cans around the room, and removing his pants. Though no specific time is given in the play, the total stage directions constitute a paragraph prior to Jon's first showing up; one imagines different theatrical versions either expanding or contracting this sequence, to prolong or condense the suspense of what Vince is up to. The film chooses the former in a scene of two minutes and forty-two seconds that emphasizes Vince's restlessness with even more energy, as he throws beer cans like a baseball pitcher or does pushups between the beds. What, exactly, is Vince preparing for? We cannot yet be sure. While narrative uncertainty alone, particularly in an opening scene, is not unusual, here such uncertainty indicates an early interest in the difficulty of knowing other people fully, much less attempting to draw out the truth of traumas either in which they have been complicit or from which they have suffered (or both). Showing an even greater sense of the difficulties in representation, the cinematography and editing move erratically, encompassing nearly every possible angle of the room while telling us very little about what is to occur. The camera often shoots the action from the ceiling or the floor as well as the bed; likewise, the editing cuts far more often than it needs to, such as using four shots to show Vince's pulling off his boots. These choices draw attention to the film as film, here underscored all the more by not being a film, exactly, but by being video, a medium that gives the images a grainy look and a more subdued color palette. Most conspicuously, a shot of Vince about halfway through the sequence doubles his image in the reflection of a television set; his placement in front of a mirror suggests further doubling. (This motif figures into later shots as well, such as when Vince first asks Jon what happened with Amy, and Jon repeats his initial answer, "We slept together," his duplicity made literal in the mirror behind him.) The reflections—and reflections within the reflections—along with the disjointed editing, the frenetic camerawork, and the washed-out video imagery indicate the film's own awareness about the exact kinds of issues raised by postmodernism. That the video is digital takes these contemporary anxieties about truth and representation even further.

Yet *Tape,* for all of its awareness of these matters, does not retreat from the past, even if its characters sometimes do, and Belber's interrogative structure often exposes the past's continued relationship with the present by examining the "seduction of lies," to use Linda Williams's phrasing, even if the truth cannot be fully excavated. Consider the first conversation between Jon and Vince, when they talk about Vince's ex-girlfriend Leah. When Jon asks for the reasons for their breakup, Vince begins with evasions ("Complicated"), then jokes ("She didn't like the way I dress"), then something closer to the truth ("She thinks I am a dick"; "She says I'm reckless"), before Vince's admission ("She thinks I have violent tendencies"). Yet this admission is hardly that—partial, indirect, and tentative, it tells us nothing of the specifics of what actually occurred. Additionally, one could read these exchanges as themselves lies, with Vince's playing the long con, trying to draw out Jon's moral superiority and condescension so that he can trap him, later, into a confession. But Jon's other comments indicate that Vince has had similar troubles in the past. When Jon asks, "What did you do?" and Vince replies, "Why do you say that?" Jon's response is, "Because I know you"; the implication is that Jon knows of comparable experiences Vince has had with previous relationships. These direct exchanges, as much as the friction produced simply by their being in the same room with one another, expose the evasions, whether deliberate or unconscious, for what they are, even if the truth is itself imperfect and incomplete. Nowhere is this more clear than in the final question of what happened between Jon and Amy, when Amy uses the lie that she has called the police to force Jon's hand; here, while it never fully reveals what, finally, happened between them, it does reveal the lies or, at least, half-truths of previous attempts to reconcile (none more demeaning than when Jon tells her, "I'm sorry you're not in a place where you can hear that right now") and simultaneously allows the trauma of the past to be felt, at least in part, by Vince, Jon, and Amy at once, rather than elided by the carefully constructed language that fills much of the conversation. (When Jon thanks Vince—"for all your honesty"—we might read that moment as genuine gratitude as much as a final ironic smirk to his friend.) Amy's lie is in a sense a mirror aimed back at other mirrors, one that exposes lies, if only within its own reflection. In *Tape* an attendance to the present means being open to such exposure so that the traumatic past may register in the tremors and shock waves sent out in the present, even if one cannot ever fully take in the originating event.

The desire to draw out the past into the present, in fact, comes not just from the interrogative dialogue but from the style itself, yet another mirror in which reflections reveal themselves. The handheld cinematography and editing adopt a larger observational approach within which one finds many variations: some shots visibly shake, while others are relatively controlled; some shots adopt odd angles, while others use more conventional ones; some shots whip quickly around the room, while others remain fairly stationary; and editing sometimes cuts unpredictably but at other times follows familiar patterns. The relatively inexpensive technologies—consumer-model cameras, Final Cut Pro editing software—lend the film a looser stylistic feel, one that evokes other cinemas that operated with lighter equipment—the Robert Drew group, John Cassavetes, Jean Rouch, the French New Wave, and other cinemas of the late 1950s and early 1960s. Such filmmakers had very different concerns but shared a sense of the camera as instrument of discovery, an association going back to the precinema experiments of figures such as Muybridge and Marey, who captured aspects of the visible world previously inaccessible through sight alone, such as a horse's feet in the air at full gallop or the anatomy of a bird in midflight. Although set in a much different context, *Tape*'s style adopts a probing, observational approach not out of keeping with this impulse of discovery, constantly altering its specific techniques as often as characters attempt to approach or deflect the events of that night from yet another angle. When Vince grills Jon on what actually happened with Amy, in a prelude to the confession, the camera uses swish-pans to record both men and the gaps between them—literally, the gaps covered in traversing the table to move from one face to another, but figuratively as well, in the history between then and now. Time and distance, too, are relevant to a later employment of this technique in two sequences, when Jon returns to apologize to Amy after having left the room. At the outset of the scene, and also later, well into the discussion, the camera moves quickly between them, from side to side, as though it might cover the distance to the past itself and bring that past into the present (Amy even says early in the series of exchanges, "I don't want there to be a communication gap here"). But the film, aware that the camera cannot collapse this inherent distance, does not linger too long in this pattern: eventually, the sequence with Jon and Vince cedes to a series of cuts, and the ones with Jon and Amy break down as well, in the second case cutting to a zoom-in on Amy's face when she says, "I was totally in love with you that night. Did you love me?" (figure 7). By shifting the technique in this latter moment in particular, the zoom, coupled with Amy's statement, does identify a truth: that Amy has felt pain and continues to when reminded of the night, even if here she seems to contradict the very confession toward which the entire film has been building. (Her later statements and actions, however, will contradict that once again.)

As it reaches its end, *Tape* is deeply ambiguous in terms of what we might expect in the future for these characters; it resists any reductive readings of their having resolved anything. But if it cannot finally provide the truth of a night ten years ago, it might allow the pain of that trauma to be revealed in the mirrors of cinema and memory. Attending to the

Figure 7. *Tape*'s handheld style: spatial and temporal distances.

present means, in this film, allowing the past to bear upon it, especially when that past involves trauma, while not reducing the complexity, even impossibility, of ever fully accounting for it or of even knowing for certain what actually occurred. In the context of postmodernism, as Linda Williams's essay suggests, mourning is always going to be a difficult, imperfect process, since the past cannot be fully represented in the present with any reliability. But if we deploy the mirrors, perhaps the past can be seen in reflection, revisited, in this imperfect way, by those who have lived it, so that the door to mourning can be left open, unlike that of the motel room that Amy closes on her way out.

In contrast to the dark ambiguity of *Tape*'s ending, however, Linklater's next project would revisit one of the most effusive and upbeat figures of *Waking Life,* Timothy "Speed" Levitch, in *Live from Shiva's Dance Floor.* Shot in the summer of 2002, once again in digital video, the roughly twenty-minute documentary follows Levitch around various locations in Lower Manhattan that converge thematically and geographically where the Twin Towers of the World Trade Center once stood, so that Levitch might propose an alternative plan for a 9/11 memorial. Giraffe Partners, a New York production company that has specialized in documentary, financed the project, the first in a series called Original Thinkers, a name taken from one of Levitch's many musings during *Shiva.* Some of Linklater's core collaborators would contribute to the film, with Lee Daniel as director of photography and Sandra Adair as editor, and when it premiered at the Sundance Film Festival in 2003, it received modest attention from at least one positive review, Su Ciampa's sympathetic "Ground Zero: Where the Buffalo Roam?" for *Salon.com.* Compared to his other work, however, *Shiva* remains one of Linklater's least-well-known films to date—partly, no doubt, due to its length, well short of most features, as well as its subject, Speed Levitch. Levitch's style of address seems to embody a cliché of the hippie almost exclusively reserved for humor in contemporary popular culture; in fact, he had previously played to that very idea in another film role as one of three stoned hippie-witches in the clever 2001 *Macbeth* adaptation *Scotland, PA.* Yet *Shiva* mitigates such potential dismissals through both the gravity of the subject matter and, at the same time, a certain levity, whether in Levitch's self-awareness about the potential risibility of his phrasings or in moments such as his sitting atop the Charging Bull statue, his legs folded, hands on each horn. This mixture of seriousness and play is in part the very attitude Levitch intends to convey in his idea for a memorial, which for Levitch as much as Linklater begins with an attendance to the present—what Levitch refers to as the "enormous now"—that must necessarily bring the past into that "now" in a way that acknowledges historical trauma, to allow for its continued mourning. (In this way, the project seems not so distant from *Tape*.) But Levitch's idea is not as abstract as this may sound; indeed, he has a very concrete proposal. And in order to explain it, he does what he has done so many times before, with visitors and locals alike: he takes us for a walk.

From the beginning, *Shiva*'s governing conceit is that of the tour, with Levitch inhabiting the role of experienced metropolitan guide, drawing up esoterica about Manhattan's history with practiced ease. He faces the camera, speaking directly to it, and his pointing to various landmarks already visible to the viewer recalls his experiences giving actual tours of the city for a double-decker bus company, which Bennett Miller detailed in his 1998 film devoted to Levitch, *The Cruise*. The cruise, or "cruising," operates not just as a description of the vehicle's ambling pace and the sense of leisure one associates with vacation; for Levitch, the notion carries erotic connotations, ones heard as well in the intimacy with which he sometimes addresses his listeners. To enact "cruising," Levitch must jettison traditional touring methodologies or, at least, wed them to his own; as much as he relies on the rhetorical address of a guide, he might also, as he does in *The Cruise*, launch into a rapid, Whitmanesque catalog of literary figures who have lived in the city; reflect on the phallic nature of the Empire State Building; or ser-enade his charges with Gershwin. In *Shiva* one finds a somewhat more focused Levitch; there is, in fact, a thesis that drives the esoterica: his proposed memorial. Nonetheless, *Shiva* also exemplifies his tendency to privilege lyric over logic. For example, while speaking of Wall Street, Levitch riffs on the meaning of the word *wall*, noting that "people do have a tendency to build walls in the face of boundlessness"; later, much in the way a poem functions, this motif returns in the fences surrounding Ground Zero. He also often makes use of the lyrical, sensuous detail, as with George Washington's statue, depicting the first president's oath of office (figure 8). For Levitch, the figure's open hand reaches across history in a "declaration of the American need for intimacy," suggesting

Figure 8. *Live from Shiva's Dance Floor*: Washington's open hand.

that "this entire Wall Street [is] simply a parable telling the tale of how much George Washington needs his hand held." Viewers, particularly historians, might wince at the loose historicizing and the poetic approach, but Levitch's aim is that these odd, tangential points form a mosaic of another New York, its historical unconscious buried in the visible monuments one meets in the present. In that sense, Levitch seems to be reprising his role as dream guide from *Waking Life,* with the city itself as dreamer.

But how does one build a memorial within a living being? For Levitch, this is the dilemma, since his New York is not just "alive" in the sense that a travel brochure might describe it—a city that, in the old cliché, "pulses with life"—but lives in a much more biological sense, its pulse almost literal. In *The Cruise,* for example, Levitch first describes the city in the language of disinterested science, as an "organism" that "evolves" and "devolves," but quickly shifts the metaphor to something much more personal, even intimate, with New York a character that might drive a stormy pulp romance, a "vindictive woman" that draws Levitch only to rebuff his overtures. In *Shiva* both comparisons are abandoned in favor of another presiding metaphor, the city as mentor or spiritual guide, if not deity; New York is here the "complicated comedian" whose humor relies on a buttonwood tree, commemorating the first transaction, with

Wall Street buildings soaring above it, "to show us how much larger our illusions are than our true nature." In the scene that follows, New York is "a great teacher bestowing life lessons on a mostly slow-learning population," those related to the "creation and destruction that is the rhythm of the universe" (hence, the figure of Shiva). Although viewers might be put off or even offended by this last description as reductive in relation to Ground Zero, Levitch's aims are quite the opposite, his vision expansive. He draws here on the mythology of New York as a place that always exceeds any attempt to articulate it, both location and idea—an image constantly in flux, like cinema itself. It is, in this way, very much alive (or is at least made to seem so, through Levitch's tour), and in order to think about how he might design a new memorial within this living space, he must return to other memorials already at work, so that the film might slowly triangulate a course toward the eventual proposal.

Through the film's relatively brief length, *Shiva* visits many kinds of memorials, including those of the more official variety, such as the Washington statue at Federal Hall or Hamilton's tomb at Trinity Church Cemetery. The uninterested people walking in and out of the frame remind us how memorials can become buried with time, merely part of the scenery. Levitch reworks those associations so that they seem to return to their original function of historical signification, even as he challenges official histories with his meandering style. And while one might disagree with his interpretations, his approach asks the viewer to confront history as it appears in all of its ragged, contradictory details, as well as those aspects of it that remain forever hidden. Accompanying these visits to more official sites, helicopter shots of the city bookend the film, demarcating beginning and ending in a familiar convention and reminding us how much popular culture once relied upon the Twin Towers as the city's most identifiable features, jutting out of the larger iconic skyline. In *Shiva* this image serves as its own memorial for what is gone, an absence that the film also echoes in its many shots of the Ground Zero site, often obscured by fences and material designed to block visitors' seeing into the construction, making the point that while the absence is clear from above, here on the ground, it remains blocked from view, a more dangerous proposition of total erasure the film wants to resist. To the extent that a nation's flag might serve a historical, even memorial function, the American flag also often appears in the background of shots; one of Linklater's favorite recurring visual motifs, not only is it part of the director's ongoing dialogue with the idea of America (whether in subUrbia, The School of Rock, Inning by Inning, A Scanner Darkly, or other films), but its appearance also calls to mind the many images of the flag witnessed in the days after 9/11, a ubiquity revealing fortitude and, at the same time, indeterminacy, the destiny of its country unfixed, a notion unsettling, perhaps, but potentially open to its more utopian promises. And the film visits two other memorials of an impromptu variety: one, an "altar" made by the workers of Ground Zero at the site itself; the other, a series of T-shirts, badges, and other paraphernalia hung on a wall nearby. Both memorials echo some of the most familiar images that have circulated around 9/11, the photographs and televised shots of the makeshift shrines that appeared following the towers' collapse, whether to commemorate lost loved ones, to find those still missing but presumed alive, or to allow for grief in the painful in-between state that many occupied in the immediate aftermath. Yet Levitch's concerns with both are that they are located at disorienting, busy locations; "There are some things in life, things like contemplation and feeling, for which you need stillness," he observes in front of the second shrine, as passersby constantly walk in front of him and confirm his sense that neither of these memorials, while fascinating in themselves, functions yet to provide that place of stillness, a sacred space even, within the metropolis (of the Ground Zero altar, riffing off of Thoreau's phrase "quiet desperation," he notes that "it's loud, it's loud"). By visiting these sites, Shiva attempts to open the viewer to new ways of thinking of older memorials, so that it might put forward a new approach to one still being conceived. The specifics of Levitch's plan, on first examination, are every bit as unusual as his lyrical digressions throughout the film: a "joy park" of roughly sixteen acres, to be filled with animals associated with a much longer history in the United States, the American bison. But in making such a seemingly preposterous suggestion, Levitch is asking us to do something not always required of us: he is asking us to use our imaginations.

The word imagination has such a childlike connotation that it is often avoided altogether in serious conversation. Yet what this park intends to offer is a place that would allow for imagination to shape our lives in ways we do not always leave room for—in part, simply by demonstrating that such a counterintuitive idea is within the realm of what is possible.

This faith in imagination might make this film, of all of Linklater's, one of his most romantic. Writing in his "Director's Statement" about the proposals already put forward, Linklater notes, "Maybe an entirely new way of looking at the issue was what was needed. What the hell—so many of the things we take for granted and enjoy as part of our lives were initially crackpot ideas the establishment scoffed at." For Linklater, the failure of the Ground Zero proposals thus far was not so much that they were bad ideas in themselves but that their original context had been so badly dreamed, leading to a basic impoverishment of creativity. New media theorist Gregory L. Ulmer has noted that *The 9/11 Commission Report* reflects on the need for "bureaucratizing the exercise of imagination." "The immediate context," Ulmer explains, "is concern that security experts had not foreseen the scenario of the hijack attacks, despite many contextual signals." If imagination were bureaucratized, the argument goes, it might lead to a better predictive political and military apparatus. But for Ulmer, this definition of imagination is flawed from the outset, since "the wording in the Report suggests a misunderstanding about imagination, as if it were a way to eliminate surprise, when the reality is just the opposite." Levitch challenges our imaginations to grow as expansive as the acres he intends to give over to the buffalo by presenting us with this unusual proposal, one that surprises in the best possible sense.

In so doing, *Shiva* encourages a state of mind that is open to such experiences, the film reintroducing us to the present tense of this city, a dynamism both real and a function of its mythology as something exceeding representation. It also attempts to show how the rich contradictions of the past, buried in landmarks the city's inhabitants pass every day without necessarily noticing them, might be brought to the surface once again, so that, as we recognize the complexities of the past—as we imagine them—we might, simultaneously, imagine a future beyond our current capabilities, past and future intersecting in the present, evoking Thoreau's "meeting of two eternities, the past and future, which is precisely the present moment" (10). What this grand act of memorializing intends to do is create a space of mourning, where we might linger on the events of that day so as to grieve and reflect in a space where other living creatures roam. Surely, Levitch's choice of animal calls to mind the famous song wherein they do just that (as in the title of Ciampa's review), but they also indicate a longer-reaching historical significance, the abatement of the animal in the United States as well as the Native American cultures that depended upon it, a connection Levitch makes explicit in his desire to put the bison "existentially front and center." This gesture, however, is not intended to supplant the events of 9/11; instead, *Shiva's* proposal is attempting something larger, to allow us to grieve the specificity of what occurred at Ground Zero while acknowledging the existence of other historical traumas that may yet be grieved. They need not cancel each other out; there is room enough in the city for these traumas and so many others. But if there is room for trauma, then there is room for its mourning, and if that is the case, then there may also be room for rethinking our past, both recent and more distant, in more rich, complex ways, by attending to a present itself more rich and complex. In so doing, we might, as we end our walk through New York City the place and New York City the idea, begin to look toward the future with something that this extraordinary act of the imagination might generate as well: hope.

Hope, or at the very least levity, characterizes the next three films that Linklater would direct, two multiplex comedies and, between them, an arthouse sequel.

For Those about to Rock, Late Afternoon in Paris, and Remixing a Little League Season

Linklater's next film begins with a deceptively simple anecdote that belies the difficulties of script development: in this case, a recurring image that screenwriter Mike White had of his neighbor Jack Black. White had previously penned a script for producer Scott Rudin, *Orange County* (2002), about a would-be college student whose brother Black had played. In thinking about another feature for Rudin, the writer returned to a notion that captured both Black's obsession with music and his childlike persona, one he later described as "this idea about him jamming around with a bunch of kids" (*"The School of Rock* Handbook"). When White had a more polished screenplay, Rudin approached Linklater, who initially declined the project, but after meeting with White, Rudin, and Black, the director signed on to the film for Paramount Pictures. From the outset, Linklater's desire for authenticity guided the production process, no matter how far-fetched the premise of a substitute teacher who forms a secret rock-and-roll band with his class; real musicians, for example, would play the parts of students, rather than actors who might only pretend to know their instruments. His normal insistence on rehearsals led to preparations for the acting and the music itself, as the musicians learned to work with one another, and once production began, shooting took place at Wagner College in Staten Island, for the school's exterior, and Buckley Country Day School in Long Island, for its interior. Costing $35 million, Linklater's highest budget to date, the film would open domestically on October 3, 2003, and would make $19.6 million in its first weekend, putting it at the top of the box office. Additionally, it enjoyed a very warm critical reception. Viewed now, with its outsider protagonist, love for popular music, antiauthoritarian sympathy, allusions, and humor, the film seems like a clear fit with the rest of Linklater's work, even as it represents a break as well, at least with the immediate past, given how little it resembles *Waking Life, Tape,* or *Live from Shiva's Dance Floor.* That Linklater's film, and the two that follow, should seem both inevitable and surprising speaks to the genuine pleasures that his career path, if not cinema history in general, always seems capable of delivering. This leads us, then, to Dewey, who is likely smirking off-camera at these reflections, as the rock-and-roll-obsessed protagonist of *The School of Rock* (Baumgarten; Macor 304–5; *"The School of Rock* Handbook").

From the outset—typically where the "inciting incident" of script-writing manuals sets the plot in motion—*The School of Rock*'s Hollywood origins are evident in its efficient narrative. Almost immediately, Dewey is kicked out of his band and threatened with eviction, and both of these events lead to his taking the job at Horace Green. More broadly, the film uses a basic three-act structure: act 1 sets up Dewey's new job, act 2 introduces complications (e.g., Summer's resistance, the principal's rules against field trips, and Dewey's termination), and act 3 builds to the climax of the "one great rock show" Dewey had promised all along. An epilogue finds order restored to the official school, with Dewey gone, but also finds the students continuing to work with both Ned and him at an afterschool program, the School of Rock. Characters, too, undergo change over the course of the film, with Dewey becoming more selfless, Ned becoming more assertive, the shy students finding self-confidence on the stage, the parents reconciling with their kids, and even the tightly wound principal loving the performance. In *The Way Hollywood Tells It,* David Bordwell explains how these conventions, including three-act structure, character arc, and others, have come to govern Hollywood screenplays. According to Bordwell, these ideas "did not overturn classical Hollywood dramaturgy" so much as "filled it in, fine-tuned it, left less to trial and error," so that, "in the 1970s screenwriting became an academic enterprise—not only because it was studied in colleges, but also because, like nineteenth-century salon painting, it was characterized by rigid rules and a widely accepted canon" (34). In light of this, we might view *The School of Rock* as among the most classical in Linklater's body of work to date—narratively, at least—and here that description takes on even more meaning, given its central character's own obsessions with the history and conventions of the subject that most fascinates him, rock and roll.

In *The School of Rock,* rock and roll is, at least initially, more a relic of the past than an ongoing cultural form in the present. The opening performance of No Vacancy's "Fight," while presumably written by a contemporary band, channels 1980s metal songs in its falsetto chorus and finger-tapping solos; the club's relative emptiness suggests not only that the group is unpopular but that rock's moment has itself passed. And just as rock's moment has passed, Dewey's seems to as well. An early shot in his room shows him lying back on his mattress, over which hangs a banner reading "Black Sabbath," in tribute to the 1970s heavy metal band, and around which scores of LP records line shelves, a technology outmoded for most casual listeners. His costume, also, works to associate his character with an earlier moment; the frequently worn bowties, for instance, belong to a previous decade more than this one. And although these clothing and accoutrements jibe with a hipster investment in vintage styles, they also underscore Dewey's devotion to rock as something very much of the past, an emphasis carried even further by the soundtrack. Unlike *Dazed and Confused,* where the soundtrack seems to pour organically from the same time period the characters inhabit, cues mostly come here from eras that predate the contemporary setting, whether 1960s and early 1970s rock like Cream, the Who, or Led Zeppelin, or precursors and practitioners of the later punk movement, like the Velvet Underground, Jonathan Richman &

the Modern Lovers, the Clash, or the Ramones—still older than the students by fifteen years or more. But of all the bands, none dominates the definition of rock more for this film than the image and music of AC/DC. One of the first songs Dewey teaches his lead guitar protégé, Zack, is "Highway to Hell"; "Back in Black" plays over Dewey's initial instrument assignments; and iconic AC/DC guitarist Angus Young shows up again in the rock-history montage, as Zack watches. The film then carries this thread through to the climactic performance of "School of Rock," where the opening guitar riff echoes AC/DC's "For Those about to Rock" (a song Dewey previously quoted when he told the students, "We roll tonight, to the guitar bite, and for those about to rock, I salute you"), and Dewey extends Young's legacy through his signature school-boy uniform, Gibson SG guitar, and wild gesticulations during his solo (figure 9). The film's ecstatic finale also begins with the competition encore number, AC/DC's "It's a Long Way to the Top (If You Wanna Rock 'n' Roll)," which plays over the credits performance, Ned and Dewey's apartment now transformed into the School of Rock. AC/DC might seem a strange choice for this film initially, given the explicit sexuality of their lyrics (an aspect the film wisely avoids), but they work well here for a few reasons. Joe Bonomo, in his book on the band's 1979

Figure 9. Dewey references AC/DC in the competition performance of *The School of Rock.*

album *Highway to Hell,* describes AC/DC's having "achieved Rock & Roll Platonism with the album" through its "'Rockness' of rock & roll" (105), an idea that this film seems to apply to the entire late-1970s and early-1980s AC/DC catalog as the culmination of what rock can do at its best. Another reason, of course, might be economic: AC/DC is one of the most popular and profitable rock bands of all time, and while the film criticizes MTV directly—a holding of Viacom, which also owns Paramount—its foregrounding AC/DC would draw their fans to theaters. Finally, it might simply be that many of the band's songs, easily played and easily taught, appeal to the educational ethos of the film generally, even if capturing that particular sound—or playing any song well, for that matter—is far more difficult in practice.

Yet AC/DC is an interesting choice for another reason as well, because, although they stand in initially for rock as a relic of the past, as the film progresses, the band's music, and rock more generally, becomes more and more a dynamic object to be engaged with in the present, one that teacher and students approach with reverence, to be sure, but also with a sense of excitement and exploration, perhaps as AC/DC themselves once relied upon older forms to create a sound for their own moment. Reflecting on this aspect of the band via email, Bonomo told me, "There's something in the blend of personalities, humor, the way they tap into a [rock-and-roll] song's elemental ingredients while finding a good hook, their celebration of pleasures, and their ordinary looks that allowed AC/DC to remake (one style of) [rock and roll] in their image, thereby making it new again." In a sense, the evolution of the central performance in this film posits a similar interaction—taking older rock sounds and forms and making them new, demonstrated in the blend of riffs and styles in the closing number, as well as the varied costumes the students wear, evoking both specific rock figures and more general rock attitudes. But the primary way that *The School of Rock* engages with a shift from past to present is through one of the most important skills it advocates: listening. When we first meet him, Dewey is incapable of listening; in his first show, he motions to the sound mixer to turn up his own guitar track, more focused on his own sound than that of anyone else. Hence, his less-than-subtle face-plant sets up his character arc, as he moves toward greater selflessness—but also better listening. His early interactions with the students are often characterized by silence, as they sit in the classroom, waiting for him to speak, or vice versa; only when he has his early epiphany, one based on his being attuned to his students playing in music class, does the dynamic in the classroom begin to change. Early in the new lesson plan, the students ask him to play the song for the contest, and the camera, in one of the most noted shots of the film, pulls back in a long take. The slow movement and silent students indicate that they are learning how to listen, even if Dewey still has a distance to go. But later we see that Dewey has made progress, as when, noticing Zack's song by listening to what is happening in the back of the classroom, he asks to hear it, eventually deciding—collectively, *with* the students—that this should be the song that they play, "School of Rock." There, too, the parent-student conflicts, muted as they are relative to the central quest to play the one great rock show, are resolved when the parents are able to listen to the song. The ending jam session is the culmination of listening, with Dewey directing various solos and improvisations, all listening to one another as they trade off, goof around, and generally have some fun. In this film, being attendant to the present is about listening to the present moment, literally and figuratively, as they explore the way the past inflects that present and as they reach toward greater self-discovery. And because the film posits these ideas as actual lessons within an educational context, it also raises at least one other body of concerns as well.

Consider, for the moment, this alternative description of the film. An iconoclast sets up shop within a classroom, only to dismantle its very structure in favor of an alternative curriculum, sowing "resistance" within his students. The whole takes place under a sense of secrecy, hidden from parents and administrators. The plot sounds like a caricature of what happens in a humanities classroom at the university level, and some might read Dewey's expulsion from the official institution as a cultural fantasy about how to deal with those troublemaking professors from the liberal arts and social sciences. My own sense of the film, however, is that it advocates quite the opposite: that it celebrates what can occur in the context of a humanities classroom at its best, whether at the college level or earlier, and despite the general anarchy of the approach here. Mark Slouka, writing for *Harper's*, has decried the decline of humanities education in our educational system, noting the "quiet retooling of American education into an adjunct of business, an instrument of production" (32). While few would argue the importance of employment or a thriving economy, business's role as the sole justification for education raises significant problems, notably the "downsizing [of] what is most dangerous (and most essential) about our education, namely the deep civic function of the arts and the humanities" (33). And why might the humanities provide this above all? "Because," Slouka answers,

> they complicate our vision, pull our most cherished notions out by the roots, flay our pieties. Because they grow uncertainty. Because they expand the reach of our understanding (and therefore our compassion), even as they force us to draw and redraw the borders of tolerance. Because out of all this work of self-building might emerge an individual capable of humility in the face of complexity; an individual formed through questioning and therefore unlikely to cede that right; an individual resistant to coercion, to manipulation and demagoguery in all their forms. The humanities, in short, are a superb delivery mechanism for what we might call democratic values. There is no better that I am aware of. (37)

This might strike many readers as absurdly grandiose in a film where the teacher instructs his students on how to "melt some faces" with the awesome power of their rock—and where the same teacher plies the school principal with beer, Stevie Nicks, and a serenade of the theme song to the television show *Good Times* (1974–1979). But the classroom scenes, at their best, enact in their own way the ambitions that Slouka outlines. They may not be exclusive to this film—one need not look far in cinematic depictions of classroom epiphanies and student growth to find similar tropes, such as the introverted student who becomes more assertive, the loudmouth who learns humility, and the incendiary nature of the material being taught. But *The School of Rock* uses these conventions effectively within its own passionate discourse about rock and roll. When Dewey, in one scene, exhorts his students to tell him what rock is "really about," he is not only instructing them on the fundamental rebellious spirit of rock, but also demonstrating, at the same time, what the humanities can do at their best: challenge and even surprise us, as when he kicks over a desk and gives exaggerated bows, demonstrating rock's theatricality and evoking laughter. The sense of the classroom as place where the past is to be performed and interrogated in the present thus shifts the educational emphasis from something static to something much more dynamic, moving from preservation to invention (or showing how the latter often partakes of the former, and vice versa). As it does so, it demonstrates what can happen in a humanities experience as something that can "expand the reach of our understanding," to borrow Slouka's phrase, the way a line of poetry, or a film's close-up, or a single note extended on a guitar solo might cause something to shift in those who read, see, or hear it, opening them outward, toward a greater sense of interaction with the world, one based on discovery and listening. Jeff Reichert, in his engaging piece on *The School of Rock,* reflects on these and so many other lessons that the film offers: "'Sticking it to the man' may be the film's oft-repeated raison d'être, but speaking softly in the background is a narrative about collaboration and teamwork, participation, discovery, and of course, playing one great show." That the film's arguably real "great show" should come in the credit sequence, after many filmgoers have risen from their seats to leave, is a final nod to the way that a humanities education should extend outside the classroom, whether school is in session or not. If this should also be very funny and tremendous fun at the same time, then part of the lesson may lie there, too, even (especially?) for books such as this one. Sometimes, *The School of Rock* suggests, we need not take ourselves so seriously. I can imagine no better final lesson than that one from Dewey Finn.

When *The School of Rock* showed at the Toronto International Film Festival in September 2003, Linklater would already be on the set of his next film, in Paris, where he traveled to find out what had become of Celine and Jesse in the nine years since *Before Sunrise.* The idea for a sequel of sorts had been percolating among director and lead actors almost since the release of the first film, the premise fairly straightforward: what happens six months later? As time went by, however, and months stretched into years, the feasibility of a December meeting became less tenable, though all three would continue to wonder about the characters' fate. These speculations led to the *Waking Life* appearance, where the couple would resume their easygoing musings and provide some momentary wish fulfillment, as we discover where they might have ended up: in love, and in bed. But the transience of the scene, combined with its narrative ambiguity, left the door open for a more concrete reunion, one that Linklater, Delpy, and Hawke set about producing in earnest.

After making a more formal outline, the three wrote collaboratively, often via email, sending large sections of dialogue to one another and slowly working their way toward the single-afternoon plot they would eventually create. Once script and financing were in place, a brief two weeks of rehearsals preceded a similarly brief three-week shoot, Lee Daniel again working as cinematographer (*"Before Sunset* Production Notes"). Some months later, on February 10, 2004, *Before Sunset* premiered internationally at the Berlin Film Festival, where Linklater had won the Silver Bear for *Before Sunrise* in 1995, a homecoming of sorts that preceded the film's general release in the summer of 2004 as the first film from newly formed Warner Independent. Scanning some of the English-language review headlines of that summer, one quickly gains a sense of the enthusiasm that greeted the film, whether in the succinct "Romantics Win: *Sunset* Follows *Sunrise*" (*Philadelphia Inquirer* [Rea]), the inviting "Be Seduced by a Sunny Afternoon in Paris" (Montreal's *Gazette* [Griffin]), the casual "Love That Goes with the Flow" (London's *Sunday Telegraph* [Marshall]), the hyperbolic "A Love Story to Send You into Swoons of Giddy Delight" (*Bath Chronicle*), and the wry "Minds That Make Out" (*Toronto Star*). In addition, Linklater was enjoying other positive attention that year: the online journal *Reverse Shot* held a "Linklater Symposium," the Cambridge Film Festival had a retrospective on his work, and the Criterion Collection released a two-disc version of *Slacker* with accompanying director commentaries and other supplements. Six years later, *Film Comment's* 2010 "50 Best Films of the Decade" list, compiled by soliciting votes from "an international poll of critics, programmers, academics, filmmakers, and others" ("A Decade in the Dark" 26), would rank *Before Sunset* at number 20 of films released in the years 2000–2009, a sure sign that so many viewers place it, as I do, among the best of Linklater's work to date.

For all of its romantic associations, *Before Sunset* has a mournful, almost elegiac undercurrent, one that derives in large part from the time that has been lost between its characters, time that cannot be recovered, no matter how hopeful one reads the ending to be. In Julie Delpy's opening song, "An Ocean Apart," a narrator mourns the loss of a relationship even as it is being lived: "Now we are together, sitting outside in the sunshine," she sings. "But soon we'll be apart, and soon it'll be night at noon." The narrator is so fixed on time's inevitable march forward that she cannot even enjoy what pleasures the relationship currently allows, as she eventually laments, "Time goes by, and people cry, and everything goes too fast." A romantic, leisurely montage of uncrowded Parisian locales accompanies the music, and these locations anticipate those that Jesse and Celine will visit as the film unfolds. The series recalls the end of *Before Sunrise,* where multiple shots showed where the couple had just been, a trace of their presence still visible in the wine bottle and glasses abandoned in the park, but whereas those images followed the chronology of the narrative and came at its end, here, they precede the action and appear in reverse, beginning with the penultimate setting of the film, Celine's courtyard, and working backward to the first, the bookstore, where they will meet. The film thus softens the potentially overwhelming sense of time's loss by simply planting this early reversal in temporal order, gently defamiliarizing any overly rational approach to time. That the payoff for this should only come later, when we have seen enough of the film to make this connection, only underscores the film's investment in the subject of time even further, one that continues as Jesse fields questions from the people gathered at Shakespeare and Company following his reading. After charmingly deflecting queries about the book's reflecting his own experiences—titled, appropriately, *This Time*—Jesse describes his next project, and Celine walks out from behind a bookshelf so that he can see her. (The moment is the first of three that open this text.) The film, however, has already revealed Celine in flashback, appearing either in relation to Jesse's comments on *This Time,* where her presence suggests its plot hews more closely to the night in Vienna than Jesse is willing to admit here, or indirectly, as when a shot of her twirling around is juxtaposed with Jesse's description of a character dancing in his next novel. These moments confirm Jesse's appropriation of Thomas Wolfe's "To the Reader," which opens *Look Homeward, Angel* by acknowledging that "all serious work in fiction is autobiographical" (xvii); they also productively blur the line between narrative time and real time, fabrication and memory, so that a meeting that never took place can be imagined in the space of Jesse's book, a fictional reunion that sparks an actual one, which Jesse later admits was his desire all along. But these moments also get to the heart of the film's ideas about time, particularly when we first see Celine some nine years later. On the one hand, and most important, Celine and Jesse have aged, just as the actors have, an effect the flashbacks highlight and one the film will take up explicitly later, at the café. But the scene also works against this sense of time's inevitable forward movement. Jesse, for example, says that "time is a lie" and that "inside every moment is another moment, all . . . happening simultaneously," which Celine's appearance seems to confirm as she steps out from behind a bookcase, time traveling from the last film to this one—or existing, in Jesse's terms, in both films at once. She makes this leap through one of the most common editing techniques in cinema, the cut, which moves us in an instant from the summer of 1995 to that of 2004 (or 1994 to 2003, if one dates the diegetic time by the shooting of the film rather than its release); the image preceding the cut is the moment from *Before Sunrise* when Jesse tries to "take [a] picture" of Celine with his mind, so that he might create a future memory, only here that memory propels us immediately forward, into the future of this moment, in the bookstore. Are we in the "now" of the first film or the "now" of the second, if not also whatever "now" we happen to inhabit whenever we see the film again and find, as Jesse does, that "inside every moment is another"? The subtle density of the marvelous cuts back and forth between both films in this opening creates a space for these reflections; it also illustrates the productive working relationship between Linklater and Sandra Adair as clearly as anything in their films to date. Shifting effortlessly from past to present to future and back again, visually, aurally, and narratively, the sequence sets up the film's primary preoccupation with time, one that characterizes time as loss, in both its inescapable progression forward and a constant looking backward, over one's shoulder, at lost days and missed opportunities, but also as mysterious and unpredictable in what it might afford—still moving forward, but yielding a potential richness all the same. (Michael Joshua Rowin, whose excellent "Mortal Beloved" also explores its interest in time, including its self-conscious opening, has put this as "the moment's finitude as well as its fullness," a useful phrasing for this temporal duality.)

Enabling these varying attitudes toward time is movement itself, in the form of walking, which constitutes so much of what these characters do in a single afternoon and leads them to various brief stops, including a café, a park, a tour of the Seine, a ride in a car, and finally, Celine's apartment. Not only does this allow for a much looser approach to dialogue, with various threads introduced, dropped, and picked up later or ignored, informing one another directly, tangentially, or not at all, the perambulations of the central couple also resonate with this particular city, Paris, site of so many aesthetic and political wanderers of the past three centuries, particularly in the figures of the dandy, the flaneur, and the surrealist. (Lesley Speed has argued for the connections between flaneurism and the "linking of urban spaces to contemplative freedom" in many of Linklater's locales, Parisian or otherwise ["Possibilities" 105].) For these and other similar figures, the Paris streets were charged with the possibility of chance encounters, ones that, for the surrealists especially, could lead to new ideas that the artist's self-consciousness might obscure. Automatism became central to their methods, whereby the artists would create strict rules for themselves, thereby outflanking the ego and encouraging chance connections they might otherwise ignore; their interest in automatism went hand in hand with an interest in automatic technologies, such as photography and cinema. Film scholar Robert B. Ray, who has seen in surrealism important connections to cinema history and new potential methodologies for cinema scholarship, has described, for example, André Breton's using automatism in the composition of *Nadja,* a method he "had begun to see . . . less as an end in itself than as a means of gathering raw material—the startling image disclosing unexpected information, the accidental meeting that transformed an October afternoon" (76). While Celine's presence at the bookstore is hardly an accident—and while *Before Sunset* is not *Un Chien Andalou*—an acknowledgment of the power of contingency, coupled with the film's interest in walking, informs this film's journey, those Parisian aesthetic movements hovering in the background of the romantic reunion (recall as well that Celine had been reading a Bataille collection on the train in the first film). Also informing this film's journey is a related investment in specific details, those that resist immediate incorporation into a larger gestalt. Consider Celine's description of her childhood walk to school:

> When I was a little girl, my mom told me that I was always late to school. One day she followed me to see why. I was looking at chestnuts falling from the trees, rolling on the sidewalk, or ants crossing the road, the way a leaf casts a shadow on a tree trunk—little things. I think it's the same

with people. I see in them little details so specific to each of them that move me and that I miss and will always miss. You can never replace anyone because everyone is made of such beautiful specific details.

As she goes on to describe specific aspects of Jesse from their first meeting—the way his beard looked in the sunlight, for example—her discussion anticipates the attentive cat in the courtyard, the one who "looks at everything like it was the first time," and also recalls a previous scene at a café, when Celine asks Jesse if she looks different than she did the last time they met, nine years earlier. Jesse replies that he remembers her as a "skinnier, I think—a little thinner," and when posed the same question, Celine comments on a crease on Jesse's forehead—"You have this line," she notes, pointing at his face. Of course, in both cases, the observations are based on the performers' aging, with an actual small line visible in Ethan Hawke's brow, a reminder of his own growing older, if not also, indirectly, the time lost between their seeing one another. In spite of that impulse, however, Celine and Jesse do not rush their investigations of the past—recounting the memories of their first encounter, as well as what they have been up to in the intervening years—and, as they wander unhurriedly through the streets, exist within the specificity of *this* afternoon, so that, in part through their attention to detail, time becomes not just loss but something else as well. What it becomes, or might become, is also suggested in the final scene, equally compelling and subtly delivered as the first, as the two arrive at Celine's apartment.

One of the most powerful moments in this final scene occurs immediately following Celine's waltz, when she walks into the kitchen to brew some tea as Jesse makes his way to her bookshelf and CD collection, pausing, as he does so, at a series of photographs on the wall. "Is this you?" he asks, "little cross-eyed Celine?" with the camera cropping the image so closely that it occupies the entire frame (figure 10). Two other photographs follow of Celine with her grandmother. The progression here is from child to older child to adult, thirty years or so collapsed into a few seconds (much like the cuts at the bookstore), encapsulating both time's more mysterious qualities and a sense of its fleeing ever onward—particularly since, once again, as in the aging discussions at the café, time's progression exists for both character and actor, since we can verify two of the photos to be Julie Delpy, younger and older,

Figure 10. "Little cross-eyed Celine": the use
of photographs in *Before Sunset*.

through physical likeness. (That we cannot with the youngest child recalls the discussion of Benedict Anderson from *Waking Life*.) And here, at last, we also see a figure that has by now taken on an almost mystical presence: Celine's grandmother, whom Michael Joshua Rowin refers to as "the overseeing spectre of *Before Sunset*," noting that her death prevented their meeting in Vienna, which also brings to mind Jesse's anecdote from *Before Sunrise* about seeing his great-grandmother in the "spray of mist from a sprinkler." These connections also extend to the first film's dedication, to Linklater's grandparents, and crop up in this film, in the bookstore, when Jesse playfully quotes his own grandfather. But Celine's grandmother, as Rowin wisely points out, assumes a central role for both characters. When Celine meets Jesse for the first time, she is returning from visiting her grandmother, and early on in the same film, Celine admits her close relationship with her grandmother, based on her sense that she is herself an old woman, about to die and dreaming her life, an image that runs from that film through *Waking Life* and into this one, where Celine and Jesse make reference to it and where it also returns indirectly, through Celine's vivid memories of her grandmother's physical presence in the coffin. The only time we see her grandmother is here, in the photograph, and the intermingling of time, death, dream, and memory in the photograph of the grandmother acts to pull these various subjects into the final scene as it also draws on older associations of the medium with mortality, whether in the writings of André Bazin, whose famous "mummy complex" compared photography to practices of "embalming the dead" (9), or those of Roland Barthes, who once reflected, "If photography is to be discussed on a serious level, it must be described in relation to death. . . . Each reading of a photo, and there are billions worldwide in a day, each perception and reading of a photo is implicitly, in a repressed manner, a contact with what has ceased to exist, a contact with death" (356). Celine's grandmother in these photographs, appearing in a medium associated with death, seems paradoxically brought to life once again, even if her presence likewise reminds us of the inevitable mortality that she has already met and that Celine and Jesse, if not the audience as well, must one day face.

Yet the film, for all this, ends with an undeniable note of joy, one that does not suppress the material fact of death, if not also time's relentless movement forward, so much as acknowledge that fact and, indeed, celebrate it, the present never quite able to rid itself of time's movement or the weight of the past, but perhaps able to offer something even greater in return. Jesse puts a song on the stereo, which Celine begins singing and dancing to, imitating the now deceased singer Nina Simone, here brought back to life through the automatic technology as well as Celine's memory of Simone's performance, a past experience remembered and making a new moment here in the present. In fact, this temporal illusion is amplified even more by the song itself, where the sounds of a "live" audience's applause, coupled with Celine's descriptions and movements, conflate present and past, so that we really do seem to be dreaming these memories as much as living them, moments within moments. Playful and warm, the whole performance, in fact, is based on Linklater's own memory of Delpy recalling the story for him, as they were planning the film: "I was staring at her across the room, sitting on the couch, and I thought, Damn if that isn't beautiful. If you're falling in love with her that would be the final look" (Koresky and Reichert). Time may continue moving forward, but the implied promise of that final scene, with Celine dancing, Jesse laughing, and Simone's voice swelling as the image fades, is that, as Linklater says, they are falling in love, a promise of renewability in the present in spite of one's mortality, a rare gift that life sometimes offers us—a gift that, in its own way, cinema might offer, too, every time we fall in love again with film, every time, to appropriate the late Pauline Kael, we lose it at the movies.

As the reverie in Celine's apartment died down, Linklater had already been at work on his next project, an adaptation of Philip K. Dick's novel *A Scanner Darkly*, but a lengthy postproduction process left him open in the latter part of 2004 to direct a mainstream summer feature about one of his own first loves, baseball, in *Bad News Bears,* a remake of the 1976 Michael Ritchie Little League comedy. When Linklater signed on to direct the film, star and screenwriters were already in place. This arrangement might, as with *The School of Rock,* seem unusual, but to dissociate him with the director-for-hire approach would be to miss something essential about his own cinephilia—namely, his love for classical Hollywood. Responding to a reporter during the publicity for *Bad News Bears,* Linklater confessed, "In my alternate universe life, I would want to be a forties or fifties studio director," citing Vincente Minnelli, Howard Hawks, and, implicitly, John Ford, when he added, "I'd love to get a call from Darryl Zanuck saying, 'Hey, we're doing *Grapes of Wrath* and you're gonna direct it'" (Houpt). In this case, Linklater took on a script authored by Glenn Ficarra and John Requa, a writing team that had produced the screenplay for *Cats and Dogs* (2001), a studio-driven kids film. More recently, the two had penned *Bad Santa* (2003), a darkly funny, very loose take on the *Miracle on 34th Street* (1947) narrative directed by Terry Zwigoff and starring Billy Bob Thornton as an alcoholic, foul-mouthed department-store Santa Claus; many reviewers commented on the affinities between that performance and his take on Morris Buttermaker, Walter Matthau's original coach. In casting other parts, Linklater would once again insist on realism, this time with athletics and especially with two key characters: Amanda and Kelly, the pitcher and slugger originally played by Tatum O'Neal and Jackie Earle Haley, and played here by Sammi Kane Kraft and Jeffrey Davies. Shooting began in Los Angeles in November 2004, and some of the core *School of Rock* personnel returned for the film, including cinematographer Rogier Stoffers, costume designer Karen Patch, and music supervisor Randall Poster. Bruce Curtis, the production designer, would become a regular Detour contributor, also serving the same role on *A Scanner Darkly, Fast Food Nation,* and *Bernie.* The following summer, on July 22, 2005, Paramount Pictures released *Bad News Bears* theatrically, and while its reviews were mixed, it nonetheless had its advocates, such as the *New York Times*'s Manohla Dargis, who praised director, writers, and lead actors for their handling of the material and equally chastised fellow critics who might dismiss a remake, noting that "Hollywood was cannibalizing its backlist before the movies started talking." Viewed against his other films, *Bad News Bears* would seem to have almost nothing to do with a sense of temporal awareness that inflects so much of Linklater's work—it is, at heart, a well-executed mainstream remake. That said, the film comes back to these ideas in a small though important sense, as it follows the season-long development of a team that loses, then wins, and then loses again.

When viewing the 2005 *Bears,* one of its most fascinating aspects is readily apparent to anyone who has recently seen the original: the close rendering of source material. Narratively, Requa and Ficarra's script creates an almost scene-for-scene reproduction of the first *Bears,* from Buttermaker's arrival at the ball field at the beginning (complete with opening a beer, pouring some out, and refilling with whiskey, enacting Amanda's nickname for him, "Boilermaker") to its ending, with the kids spraying beer over one another after losing the final game (nonalcoholic, in the new version). So closely, in fact, does the film follow the original that Bill Lancaster, who authored the first film, appears in the credits as one of the screenwriters. Stylistically, too, the film draws frequently on the original. In the opening, for example, the camera frames Boilermaker from the same side of the car, and at the end, both films similarly use long shots of the postgame celebration, American flags conspicuously framed in the foreground (figure 11). What these and many other aspects of both films draw attention to is the nature of the remake in cinema. A common form within contemporary media, and existing across both film and television (and crossing from one to the other), the remake allows studios to hedge their bets with releases calculated to draw audiences to the newer version—often with properties they already own, making them even more lucrative—and, simultaneously, create some curiosity about the original. (Commenting on the latter effect, the *Austin Chronicle*'s Raoul Hernandez joked, "A week prior to the theatrical release of Richard Linklater's *Bad News Bears* last Friday, locating an unrented copy of the original film here in the director's video-gorged stomping grounds proved as easy as getting Major League Baseball to

Figure 11. *Bad News Bears*: the final shot
cites the original ending.

pardon Pete Rose.") In his essay "Twice-Told Tales: Disavowal and the
Rhetoric of the Remake," Thomas Leitch has reflected on the desire of
remakes "to please both audiences who have seen the films on which
they are based and audiences who have not" (41), as well as a central
paradox they embody: "The fundamental rhetorical problem of remakes
is to mediate between two apparently irreconcilable claims: that the remake is *just like* its model, and that it's *better*" (44). This *Bad News Bears*
leans more toward the first impulse than the second; the remake has no
desire to supplant the first film but, rather, *wants* viewers to notice its
invocation of the earlier one, so dense and multiple are the references
to it. In this respect, it is closer to Leitch's homage, "whose primary
purpose is to pay tribute to an earlier film rather than usurp its place
of honor" (47). Narrative connections are explicit, whether in character
names (Buttermaker, Whitewood, Kelly, Amanda), character traits (Tanner's foul mouth, Engelberg's weight), events (Buttermaker's passing out
at practice, the early forfeit to the Yankees), dialogue ("booger-eating
moron," "bad news for the Athletics"), or overall structure, and visual
and aural icons abound, in Tanner's hair, the yellow jerseys, Bizet's *Car-
men* music, Buttermaker's car, Buttermaker's beers and cigars, Kelly's
motorcycle, Amanda's brushing her cap lid before a pitch (a reference
to the spitball of the first film), and specific stylistic choices such as the

long shot of Kelly's throwing the ball from just beyond left field or the cut from a shot of Kelly at practice to one of a ball sailing out of the park during a game. Unlike other remakes that attempt to trump their predecessors, *Bad News Bears* very much wants viewers to recall the first film, and it locates much of its potential pleasure in a dialogue between one's memory of the first film and one's experience of the remake (or in Linklater's words, the "remix"), a back-and-forth that mingles with those other memories, filmic and otherwise, as the movie unfolds.

Within the second film's desire to revisit the first is one of the most enduring appeals of the original: its refusal to dilute the pain of losing, whether resulting in social ostracism or simply a sense of worthlessness, that registers as an affront to America's idea of itself, a national identity often bound up in a refusal to acknowledge loss or the possibility of systemic failures that lead to it. Although the broad humor of the remake softens the theme, whether in the bus-stop bench reading "Been Laid?" or the stripper cheering section from "Bo-Peeps Gentlemen's Club," the team celebrations at Hooter's (that also function as franchise commercials) or other elements, the overall ethos of both films is still very much about losing. In both cases, the narrative is set in motion by legal action forcing an already well-structured organization to make room for another team it does not want; the wry inside joke is that, while holidays and statues are fine, any actual disruption that civil rights enforcement requires is a threat, even in the benign context of Little League baseball. From this point forward, losing will dominate both films; although the Bears win some games, the victories mostly occur in a montage, and they become undermined later by Buttermaker's growing desire for victory at any cost. The final loss may be saved in part by his act of self-abnegation, when he allows the rest of the team to play and risks the loss that the Bears eventually earn (and that he sees coming, outside some momentary hope at the bottom of the sixth inning), but despite postgame celebrations, moments of glory for individual team members, and what Liz Whitewood, in the remake, calls a "moral victory," the bluntness of loss throughout both films confirms what the kids already suspect: the system is unfair and unequal, and this loss prefigures others to come. Dana Polan, writing for the journal *Jump Cut* in 1977, said of the first *Bears* that "the film ends in pessimism; whatever positive advances the characters have undergone are inconsequential within the enormity of the world which engulfs them." Gerald Peary, writing in the same journal only an issue prior, would insist on a different reading, finding a "revolution[ary]" quality to the film, seeing "heroes and heroines" in what he describes as "the perfect microcosm of the disenfranchised." For most viewers, I suspect, the appeal of the original and the remake is in fulfilling basic narrative desires to see the Bears, with Buttermaker, eventually come together as a team and suffer a loss rendered noble, if still a loss. And of course, humor and a general desire not to take itself very seriously work against dwelling too long on these issues.

That said, Polan's and Peary's readings of the original not only illustrate the potential implications of loss, but also remind us how both *Bears* films find subtle but intriguing ways to acknowledge larger political realities. Consider, for example, the way the films treat opening day. In the original, as Kelly rides his motorcycle, following a girl he will try to impress when he jumps the fence a few moments later, we can hear an off-screen announcer saying, "Ladies and gentlemen, I want to welcome you here to the opening game of the season, out here, with your children, in the American spirit." The film cuts to Whitewood, at home plate, who is the speaker; he continues, "What I want is to see every boy, in America, out on the baseball field, playing the great game of baseball." The original's invocation of nationalism at the outset of the season reflects the same bicentennial that hovers over *Dazed and Confused* (a connection Dargis's *New York Times* review makes as well), and also ironically draws attention to the ways that America's self-image had faltered in the wake of Vietnam, a disgraced president, an unpredictable economy, and other circumstances. (Whitewood will eventually be revealed as a cynical politician, if viewers have not already identified him as such, when he attempts to talk Buttermaker into "disband[ing] the team" after the embarrassing forfeit.) Compare this scene to the way the remake handles opening day, when an emcee announces, "Because in this time of terror, there is one thing we all need: the grace of our Lord, our heroes overseas, and baseball." The line refers directly to the first-term administration of President George W. Bush, whose rhetoric implicitly framed counterterrorism as Christian crusade and appealed to sympathies for those serving in the military as a way to justify the Iraq War. While Linklater's politics are not easily assigned to either major American political party, a subject the next section will treat at greater length, he had been vocal in his opposition to a second term of Bush's presidency during the fall of 2004, when he signed a half-page ad that ran in several newspapers, also endorsed by other Texas artists, that read, "The Texan in the White House doesn't speak for us." Shooting for *Bad News Bears* had been set to begin on Monday, November 15, 2004, almost two weeks after the presidential election on Tuesday, November 2, 2004, that would reelect Bush, and the film's attempt to draw on its contemporary political reality, in however small a way, seems to extend a bridge to the first film's similar desires. Of course, not all attempts to bridge social realities work as well as others. The new *Bears*'s treatment of race, for example, attempts to capture some of the original film's more explicit treatment of the subject (most famously in Tanner's line, one the remake cuts, about a team of "Jews, spics, niggers, pansies"), but it never quite knows how to handle it, encouraging audiences to find racism either funny, as in Buttermaker's slights, or offensive, as when a racist comment starts a fight during the championship game. Still, the brief ways that the remake touches on political realities give the humor an underlying dourness, one it borrows as much from the first film as it does from its own political context.

But *Bad News* is ultimately a comedy where the humor, whether broad, as in the infield slapstick, or subtle, as in Thornton's slow-burn frustration with the kids until he grows to enjoy coaching, far outweighs its darker political implications. Instead, the film most often finds life on the ball field itself, and there is something in the pleasure of the game's smaller moments, a low-key engagement in enjoying baseball for its own sake, that does not view fun with suspicion, or competition itself as unhealthy, and that advocates the joy in the present moment of any practice or game, whether on the field or sitting in a dugout as an inning unfolds. This is where the film most closely interacts with a sense of time like other films in Linklater's work. Here, also, *Bears* draws upon the first film; Polan, again in 1977, notes how so many of Michael Ritchie's films deal with a pursuit for its own sake: "Ritchie's films applaud most those moments when people can simply enjoy something, and not have the corrupted values of others distort that enjoyment: the pure thrill of skiing in *Downhill Racer*, of flute playing in *Smile*, of ball playing in

The Bad News Bears." Although Polan views any potential "rebellion" as "limited in scope" and reminds readers that "baseball, all sports, exist in a certain social context," the finite, provisional nature of these experiences makes them all the more poignant, even in the low-stakes world of Little League baseball, a sport that Linklater himself has a personal investment in. He played baseball in college and worked many Little League games as an umpire, and the film often reflects a love of the game in its more mundane aspects as much as its pop flies and home runs. For example, one brief moment during a montage shows the kids playing "pepper," a practice activity that players sometimes use to warm up, a detail more about the specific moments within a practice than a triumphant at-bat during a game. Or consider when Buttermaker gives the team signals for a play to steal a run. The silent gestures, part of baseball's mystique, answered with nods and eye-line matches, allows viewers momentarily to inhabit a play as it unfolds, rather than simply seeing the result, as one might, for example, in a televised game. The championship, too, changes pace noticeably when Engelberg hits a home run, and while this represents a high point for the Bears, most of what is interesting in the scene is Engelberg's showy running of the bases, taking his time as he rounds third, eliciting a smile from Buttermaker. After this, of course, Buttermaker pulls Amanda from the game entirely, a nice change from the original, as the two reconcile in the dugout—the location where baseball often takes place, too, as the film makes clear. To be sure, many of the film's pleasures might be those we would ascribe to well-constructed scenes in other films of the sports genre, and the message to enjoy athletics for their own sake, without becoming too caught up in one's selfish aims, is also familiar. Nevertheless, Linklater's revisiting of *The Bad News Bears* in this film offers viewers a sense of the game's smaller moments, those that might have something to offer both athlete and spectator, however temporary, as well as the way that a team's coming together is itself ephemeral, players and coach drifting off at season's end into their respective summers. *Bad News Bears* may not dwell so concretely on temporal questions as many of Linklater's other films do, but it does take part in this dialogue, however modestly, even as it also reveals the potential limits of creating a holistic view of a career that continues to be unpredictable in the best possible way.

Little Blue Flowers and
Echoes from the Slaughterhouse

The test is simple: in one hand, a toy elephant; in the other, an identical toy elephant. The man must confirm, while not looking, only feeling, that in each hand he holds the same object. But he cannot pass the test. Try as he might, his mind is already much too far gone to make this basic connection. In the summer of 2006, audiences would follow the man, Bob Arctor, as he attempted in vain to identify the replicas of a species from another continent, in Linklater's next release, *A Scanner Darkly*. A digitally animated retelling of Philip K. Dick's novel, *Scanner* had begun years earlier, though it had not been Linklater's first choice among the author's work; the director had initially been interested in *Ubik* but had been unable to secure the rights. Then, in late 2001, Stephen Soderbergh and George Clooney's company, Section Eight, optioned *Scanner* for Linklater, so that he could set about producing a screenplay (Macaulay). The project would not pick up momentum again until 2004, when Keanu Reeves was officially cast in the role of Arctor; from that point, interest quickly built again, other actors coming aboard while two key members of the *Waking Life* team, Tommy Pallotta and Bob Sabiston, also committed. Shooting began in May of that year and wrapped six weeks later, after which time the filmmakers cut together a version that the animators could use for visual reference, much as they did with *Waking Life*. At this point, however, the production ran into problems. The animation process took much longer than expected, so much so that Sabiston, creator of the technology, was replaced as head of animation, and the original release date was pushed back from September 2005 to July 2006 (La Franco). When Warner Independent released the film that summer, its box-office performance was disappointing, though several critics took great interest in the film's use of digital rotoscoping. Whatever reasons accounted for its drawing or deflecting audiences, *A Scanner Darkly* remains a fascinating part of Linklater's oeuvre, its admiration for its novel and novelist apparent in its closely followed narrative, similarly rendered characterizations, uncannily congruent visual and aural style, and, most fleetingly if not also most directly, Dick's image interpolated briefly into one of the earliest appearances of the scramble suit.

As a Philip K. Dick adaptation, *Scanner* presents a special case. For all of its science-fiction trappings, the novel is one of Dick's most autobiographical, a collection of anecdotes drawn from his time at 707 Hacienda Way in San Rafael, California, after his wife, Nancy, had left him in September 1970, but set in Orange County, where he would eventually land in 1972, after the Hacienda Way home had been foreclosed on. (In the film, the address is 709, a numeric authorial motif Linklater has worked into so many of his films, much like American flags, pinball machines, anarchy symbols, and other signatory touches.) What followed Nancy's departure, along with their daughter, Isa, who would later be close to the film's production, was a time of Dick's residing in his former suburban home with fellow drug users, some who lived there and others who were just passing through, in an atmosphere stoked by heavy drug experimentation, the effects of which sometimes led to heightened euphoria but also, in other cases (and for Dick especially) paranoia. Several events in both novel and film come from this period, including a friend's hallucination of insects in his hair, another friend's trying to make cocaine from sunblock, an unexpected car malfunction, a suspicious break-in that seemed both to confirm Dick's theories and to cast doubt on his sanity, and a woman whom Dick was in love with and whom he once accused of being an undercover agent (Carrère 173–219; Sutin 166–207). In these and so many other ways, *Scanner* may be the closest that cinema has come to a biopic on the writer, albeit filtered through a science-fiction dystopia, and it simultaneously reflects some of Dick's most central obsessions at the time, including the rise of totalitarian state surveillance (borne out for Dick in the early 1970s by Watergate), the adopting of a paranoiac attitude in order to deal with that rise, the individual and cultural problems endemic to drugs, and the sense that meaning and reality were themselves becoming fractured and incoherent or, conversely, deceptively complete, but with something essential left out, an insight as relevant to a drug-addled brain as to a postmodernist thinker such as Jean Baudrillard, who cites Dick's writings in *Simulacra and Simulation* (Rosa 62). Michel Foucault would also have been composing his 1975 *Discipline and Punish,* where he discusses his concept of panopticism, at roughly the same time that Dick was imagining the hypersurveillance of *Scanner.* The questioning of reality, of course, has a much longer history than a cursory look at late-twentieth-century philosophy would suggest; as scholar Jenna Ng reminds us, "That the objective world might be merely an illusion is not an original proposition." Citing Plato's Cave as one of the original narratives of reality and illusion, Ng suggests that recent popular consciousness of these ideas was particularly inflected by *The Matrix* (1999), which went beyond Plato (and drew upon Baudrillard) to suggest a "reality understood not in terms of its delusion, but, rather, its more sinister simulacrum and the attendant specters of technological domination and copy/image creation. The world does not exist as objective truth, but as image and likeness" (172–73). Reeves's casting in *Scanner* nods to this context, as does a moment at the monitor banks, when Arctor/Fred downs three red pills, which recalls the color of pill that Morpheus offers Neo in the potent catalyst for his great awakening. But rather than explore the ultimately reassuring ethos of the *Matrix* trilogy—the God in the machine, and vice versa, if not also the potential for self-actualization within a world of image and likeness—*Scanner* sees its would-be prophet lost in the maze as his sanity gradually erodes, a casualty of what turns out to be a much larger conspiracy between government and private industry to keep the masses at bay, corrupting democracy and free will through a dangerous substance and then blaming the users for their own addictive ways. Bob Arctor's gradual deterioration follows this trajectory, multiplied exponentially on the almost infinite monitors, always recording, capturing nearly every movement he makes, so that he might catch himself in the process of doing something he has already done, may be doing, or may yet do.

These ambiguities are part of *Scanner*'s larger temporal obsessions, ones tied to the darker side of the present moment, closer in attitude to *subUrbia* than *Waking Life*. Writing about the novel, Christopher Palmer describes it as Dick's attempt to examine postmodernism generally as well as, more directly, the series of individual, personal losses painfully tabulated in the "Author's Note" at novel's and film's end. For Palmer, this desire to examine accounts for the novel's "steady pace." But he also relates this pacing to the characters, who experience a "slowing, and thence a nightmarish stopping of time" in their addictions, a state in which "they don't find death in the sense of an ending, but reach a stalled cessation of time and experience" (177). While the idea of deterioration implies chronological progression, and while Arctor's own takes place within a larger narrative structure, part of what the film explores is a related temporal hell of "stalled cessation," where the present is detached from past and future, but slowly dying, nonetheless, a quiet entropy its subjects can barely feel until they have gone too far past any possibility of rehabilitation, despite New Path's ostensible mission. This slowing is in contrast to the opening of both novel and film, which begin briskly, with a character desperately trying to rid himself of bugs (Jerry in the novel, Freck in the film). But as the narrative finds its way to Arctor's house—a locus for much of the plot, as it was for much of Dick's life in this period—the pace slows considerably, bearing out Palmer's observations. Consider a scene at the house where Bob, Donna, Barris, and Luckman argue over whether the bicycle that Barris just purchased is stolen, how many gears it has, if any gears are missing, where the "orphan gears" may have gone, and whether they should confront the sellers. In the text, the scene serves to illustrate a growing concern over Arctor's mental state, given his inability to figure out what the medical deputies compare to "a junior high school aptitude test" (118). But the scene's anthropological disposition, a fascination with its participants' language evident in the dialogue's presentation as transcript, slows the pacing, as does Dick's decision to interrupt the transcript periodically with excerpts from a scientific article called "The Other Side of the Brain: An Appositional Mind." The film, in turn, presents a much more immersive portrait of the characters attempting to work through the bicycle dilemma, beginning with Barris's manic "Total, total, total, totally" line. Yet the film maintains a desire to slow the narrative itself, even if the pace of conversation compensates with speed; *this is how these characters think, speak, and live,* the scene seems to say, rather than *this is how what these characters are currently doing will lead to something important later.* The dialogue over bicycle gears suspends cause and effect, past and future, in an atmosphere actually quite appealing in its humor and sympathy for its participants, so that Arctor's later hollowing out is that much more tragic, since he does genuinely seem to have lost something—not just the family he flashes back to, but also these, his friends, in the world they have created within the house. Guiding the film's sense of drift, this "stalled cessation," in Palmer's words, works on a present-ness that obscures a more coherent sense of time, where loss—of individual freedoms, of relationships, of sanity—accumulates quietly, barely noticed by those who will pay the ultimate price.

Arctor's unsteady hold on time is manifest also in a larger sense of displacement that guides both his and our experiences. The film makes its interest in displacement clear in a much larger conceit it plays with, albeit moderately: that the whole might itself be a scanner transmission. Like monitors receiving a direct but impure signal, title sequence and credits flicker, and a conspicuous, jarring transition from Barris and Freck at the diner to a fast-forward sequence, complete with horizontal bands indicating a video display, also relies on this idea, as does a later transition, when Arctor turns off a monitor and the screen goes black. More important, however, to a sense of displacement are those scenes when Arctor appears to be not only in two places at once, through his monitors, but in two times as well. Partly, the effect of simultaneity has to do with new media technologies that allow for an overwhelming amount of constantly generated information. D. N. Rodowick, attempting to describe the temporal sensibility created by such technologies, has argued that they convey "a deep immersion in the present where one struggles to control both the amount of information one receives and knowledge of how to sort, store, and retrieve it properly": in other words, an overwhelming sense of the present, where the past cannot be represented and where, as Rodowick notes, "one is always in a hurry" (176). Whether one agrees with this assessment more generally or not, it seems accurate to Arctor's experiences here, but with an exception: the deep immersion in the present becomes, instead, multiple presents, where he might inhabit more than one time at once. This occurs when he watches himself on the scanners, which, instead of conveying a sense that he is watching his actions in the immediate past, often suggests that he is watching them unfold in another simultaneous present, an alternate *now* instead of a *then*. One example of this slippage occurs in the house, when Luckman tells a story about someone who decides to become a "world-famous impostor." The person, however, realizing the work involved in being an actual impostor, opts to pretend to be one instead, becoming an impostor of an impostor, the irony of which amuses the group. As Luckman continues, the scene cuts to the scanner room, where Bob/Fred watches the scene continue, but now through the scanners. Since the sound sutures the cut, however, and since there are no other more conventional signals in the transition that we have moved ahead in time (such as a dissolve or a fade), the dialogue seems to be happening in the present rather than the past. Furthermore, when Bob uses the phrase "poses as a narc," while talking with Barris and Luckman about undercover agents, the film cuts from Bob at the house to a close-up of Bob's face in the scanner room, where he appears surprised. Although such surprise may be a lapse of memory, it also suggests a genuine reaction to something unfolding in the present, even though it has occurred in the past. Bob is losing a sense of who he is, but he is also losing a sense of *when* he is—each *now* seems viable, a paradox, like posing as a narc. (His image fractured on several monitors at once also underscores this breakdown [figure 12].) The scene where he watches the nude torso of a woman transform into Donna, and back into the stranger, also suggests multiple *nows*, given that the transformation should have been possible only in his home but recurs—or occurs in a different, simultaneous *now*—as he sees the transformation in the scanner station, monitors eroding past, present, and future so that all presents occur at once, in a jumbled mess no single mind can assimilate. One thinks again of Fredric Jameson, who has compared the temporality of postmodernity to the experience of the schizophrenic, a figure "condemned to live a

Figure 12. Multiple "nows" in *A Scanner Darkly*.

perpetual present with which the various moments of his or her past have little connection and for which there is no conceivable future on the horizon" ("Postmodernism and Consumer Society" 137).

Bob's temporal fracturing in these scenes and others attends his mental breakdown, one that leads to New Path and, eventually, a field of blue flowers, the agricultural origin of Substance D. By the end, Arctor, now Bruce, exists as an alive but dead subject who can be trusted to keep the secret of the drug, since he lives in a perfect, if horrifying, present that knows neither a past, erased from memory, nor a future—as Dick puts it his novel, "there was nothing left to happen" (275). Had the film ended here, it would have been considerably darker, and while it would be wrong to characterize the final scene as anything but mournful, we might take some solace in its remaining temporal gestures, in their attempts to bring both past and future back into the narrative, if only briefly. Bruce himself, as he tucks a flower into his shoe, remarks that it will be "a present for my friends, at Thanksgiving," a way to expose the larger conspiracy he is now helping facilitate, even if his ability to grasp the reasoning for this gesture is left ambiguous; in so doing, he reaches toward the past, in the memory of his friends, and the future, in his vague consciousness of the calendar and the Thanksgiving holiday. This moment is followed by an even greater exhumation of the past, in the film's final words, taken from Dick's "Author's Note," when a list of "people who were punished entirely too much for what they did" fills the screen, names followed by conditions such as "deceased" and "permanent psychosis," those for whom the "stalled cessation" of the present eventually overcame them. The original impulse, conveyed by the film, is not to suggest any sense of moral punishment, since, in Dick's own words, the narrative "does not say they were wrong to play when they should have toiled" but that "the punishment was far too great" (277). By including the note, however, the film reflects on the past, both that of Dick's friends and that of Dick himself, also now gone, and invites the viewers' own contemplation of others they might have lost as well, whether to addictions or otherwise. Reflecting on the importance of this ending for the film, Linklater has noted, "I said everyone who works on the film had their own list, and we all do. We all do. You can't live too long in this culture and not be acquiring your own list of casualties who you feel in an almost unfair way went way too soon" (Johnson 339). The final act of this science-fiction biographical hybrid thus becomes one of memorial, as we watch Arctor working silently and read the words that follow, the film's last transmission.

The science-fiction prophecies of Philip K. Dick would cede, in Linklater's next film, to an investigation of a business global in scale yet encountered frequently in the most mundane of experiences. Imagine, for a moment, driving at night across the United States and, having been on a fairly deserted stretch of road, seeing through the windshield the approaching lights of a town. The lights would cluster and divide as the car approached, beacons becoming several—dilating, gaining color, and growing ever more distinct. And as one entered the town, one might even stop under one such light, a multihued sign already well known and promising a meal inside that would be inexpensive, quickly prepared, and quickly consumed, so much so that the driver might even be unable to recall, later, exactly where or when the meal took place. But what if we could linger in this imaginary diversion and, like a modernist dream of an all-seeing camera, follow the light of this multihued sign in other directions—behind the counter, where the meal is prepared; back to corporate headquarters, where decisions are made; back to the suppliers, where the meal's ingredients are produced; and finally, to the workers at every step along this chain and the lives they lead, by choice, circumstance, or a combination impossible to disentangle? We might find ourselves returning to *Fast Food Nation*, Linklater's 2006 narrative film of Eric Schlosser's 2001 book-length exposé that seeks to reveal the underlying systems and material realities that constitute the fast-food industry.

The initial impetus for fiction, rather than documentary, came from Malcolm McLaren, probably most famous for having managed the Sex Pistols, and Jeremy Thomas, whose Recorded Picture Company, which had in the past produced films directed by Nicolas Roeg, Nagisa Oshima, Bernardo Bertolucci, and David Cronenberg, would serve as the production company on this film. McLaren and Thomas conceived of the project in narrative terms from very early on, a general approach that Schlosser and Linklater first discussed during the author's 2001 book tour for *Nation* through Austin. Four years later, in the fall of 2005 and with a script written by both of them, Linklater would begin filming; Lee Daniel would again serve as cinematographer, this time employing a Super-16 stock that provided a naturalistic realism to the slaughterhouse settings.

(In the intervening time, among his other film projects, Linklater had made a pilot for HBO called $5.15/Hr. [2004], a show about minimum-wage workers that would provide a context to think about some of the same issues explored in *Fast Food Nation*.) Shooting took place in Austin and other locations in both the United States and Mexico, none perhaps more poignant than a visit to the former home of "Hank," an affable rancher from Schlosser's original text who eventually, and unaccountably, takes his own life ("*Fast Food Nation* Press Kit"; Schlosser 133–47). First showing, like *Scanner*, at the 2006 Cannes Film Festival, followed by a U.S. release that November, *Fast Food Nation* received varying responses from critics, many of them less than charitable. That said, to accept some of these initial misgivings at face value would be to miss what remains one of Linklater's most powerful and unreservedly political works to date; class structure, corporate greed, immigrant exploitation, national health issues, and other concerns all come to bear on a tour-de-force indictment of American consumption and exceptionalism.

Although we might ascribe these subjects to specific political traditions, if not also specific political parties, we might also view them as appealing to multiple ideologies, broadly united in a desire to resist entrenched structures—here, the fast-food industry, franchise culture, and labor relationships—that reflects the way Linklater's work often seems palatable to more than one set of political sympathies. *Slacker*, for example, includes a conspicuous shot of a presidential-campaign billboard for Ron Paul, then Libertarian and future Republican, and Alex Jones, a political commentator also associated with libertarianism (and who, according to *Austin Chronicle* editor Louis Black, "has emerged as an international leader in the conspiracy community"), appears in both *Waking Life* and *A Scanner Darkly*. In contrast, one also finds Celine, in the *Before* films and *Waking Life*, averring a more general leftist politics, and the films as a whole often engage in an ongoing critique, progressive in nature, related to the darker side of consumerism, market economies, and the workers who make those systems possible. Many other examples, ones as different as *Dazed and Confused, Live from Shiva's Dance Floor*, and *The School of Rock*, suggest politics that reject the status quo but have no one allegiance, which is why people of varying political persuasions may find common ground—or, at least, multiple overlapping grounds—within the films, sometimes even in a single scene or character. *The Newton Boys'* Willis serves as a good example, with his ideas that are conservative (his appeals to traditional values and regional identity), progressive (his challenges to the power structure of banks and landowners), and libertarian, anarchic, or both (his disregard for legal prohibitions against bank theft). While a healthy levity often balances out the films' more didactic moments, none has come so close to direct, explicit attempts to awaken viewers politically as *Fast Food Nation,* its straightforward critique mixed with an equitable treatment of all characters and a general unwillingness to demonize a single person rather than a larger industry whose baser practices seem unchangeable—but which the film views as anything but.

In building its critiques, *Fast Food Nation* relies heavily on its source, both in the material that informs its characterizations—the chapters "Behind the Counter" for Amanda, for example, or "Cogs in the Great Machine" and "The Most Dangerous Job" for Raul, Sylvia, and Coco— and in its larger approach. Schlosser's text makes its case slowly, so that an argument takes shape gradually rather than all at once; likewise, the film accumulates details at a steady pace, so that long-held conceptions about the industry might begin to unravel over the course of roughly two hours. Also aiding the unusual adaptation from nonfiction to fiction are the book's narrative impulse, where a single person's story often anchors a greater subject, and its rhetorical strategy, where asides and digressions fill out the complexity of the system it is critiquing, a sensibility in keeping with Linklater's cinema, which often welcomes departures from a central narrative. Beyond the source text, however, many others inform the film, none more directly than one often cited by both writer and director: Upton Sinclair's book *The Jungle,* the early-twentieth-century novel about the horrors of the meatpacking industry. Although tonally different—Sinclair combines melodrama, gory detail, and socialist propaganda to spark outrage and keep it fired for the duration—the slaughterhouse scenes, especially those of the kill floor, recall *The Jungle,* and Schlosser's investigative journalism, begun originally in two *Rolling Stone* articles, is in line with the longer tradition of muckraking to which *The Jungle* belongs. In addition to Sinclair's novel, the film nods to Mark Twain when Don reads *A Connecticut Yankee in King Arthur's Court* to his sons (though the book cover references "The Celebrated Jumping Frog of Calaveras County"), and the tradition of nineteenth-century

American naturalism, with its interest in the ways larger economic and social forces shape an individual's life, is at work in the film (the spirit of Frank Norris seems to inform the whole and recalls the appearance of the Norris adaptation *Greed* in *The Newton Boys*). Structurally, the film draws inspiration from another text Schlosser and Linklater consulted prior to making the film: Sherwood Anderson's episodic *Winesburg, Ohio.* Similar to Anderson's avoidance of a single narrative in favor of several interlocking ones, *Fast Food Nation* generates three equally important plots, all driven by their own protagonists: Don, an executive for the Mickey's Corporation, a condensation of McDonald's and Walt Disney, sent to investigate the quality of meat coming from the company's suppliers in the town of Cody, Colorado, an invented location that serves as the film's main setting; Raul and Sylvia (and to a certain extent Coco), Mexican immigrants who cross the border to work in a meatpacking plant in Cody; and Amber, a bright teenager who works at a local Mickey's, also in Cody. These three narratives, commenting on one another through juxtaposition and the occasional intersection of characters, are the means by which the film gradually deconstructs the larger systems at work and the physicality of the fast-food burger itself, from its opening idyllic, commercial imagery, sun flares on the lens evoking a pastoral setting more than a manufactured one, to the final long take of patties rolling off the line.

Deconstruction requires temporal movement, of course—here, the recurring motif of Don's eating a burger becomes more and more unsettling, the more he learns—and likewise, the film's division into two halves, with the second taking place two months later, suggests a normative movement forward in time. But the film also explores a temporal mind-set of a perpetual present, particularly in the fate of two characters, Don and Sylvia. In contrast to *Scanner*'s Substance D, however, *Nation* never locates a single source for this temporal breakdown; instead, the film creates a mosaic of an industry whose influence is important but dispersed (which acts as a kind of alibi), even as we see its effects registering in both concrete, material ways and the more elusive temporalities of both characters. Don, for example, is at film's end essentially both where and when he began, introducing the "big launch" for the latest sandwich that bears almost no distinction from older ones aside from a new marketing campaign. Although Greg Kinnear's performance provides some subtle shading, indicating disaffection with his job, Don has nonetheless not essentially moved anywhere in time, stuck as he is in the temporal present of the boardroom, where the same conversations take place again and again. In a much more immediate and, as the film acknowledges, dangerous situation, Sylvia is stuck in a perpetual present, her place in the assembly line's repetitive motion a metaphor for a nightmarish forward momentum that is also stasis, where a subject both goes nowhere and burns out and where the future is elided in the rapid flow of viscera, a future that may end tragically, seen already through injuries to both Raul's friend and Raul, as well as alluded to briefly in an early shot of an amputee. The film's final images of immigrants crossing the border, children greeted with the freeze-frame of "Itty Bitty Meals," suggests as well a present-focused existence in which one is encouraged to look no further than one's immediate *now*, the accumulation of the past in the border-migration casualties—signified by a shoe in the desert and a coyote's crossing himself—ultimately invisible for so many of us (Don's absence in the latter part of the film stands in for a general desire to turn away from these realities, another concession to this present). In addition to these narratives, the film explores a similar temporality in its vision of America, an indistinct landscape of disintegrating strip malls, fast-food icons, suburban housing sprawl, apartment buildings, poor communities, and roads and highways connecting all of them. It becomes difficult in such a landscape not only to distinguish a sense of space, with regional differences erased in the design orthodoxies of franchise culture, but to distinguish a sense of time as well, since the structures that house these businesses convey a lack of history, their identity tied to the promise of instantaneity. *Nation* reminds us of this in recurring images of franchise icons; at various moments, we see a "Mart," a Precision Tune, a Papa John's, a Hollywood Video, and the fictional Mickey's. Such icons suggest not just instantaneity but also, ironically, permanence (a word Philip K. Dick uses to describe his very similar characterization of Orange County's landscape and its "neon ooze" in *Scanner* [31]), as though they have always been there, so that history is not so much repressed as it no longer seems to apply in this temporal stasis. Consider the establishing shot immediately preceding Raul and Sylvia's night out, at the outset of the second part of the film, where a caption reading "TWO MONTHS LATER" accompanies a long shot of their being stuck trying to cross a highway, fast-food icons behind them as cars race past a landscape that could belong to 2006, 1996, 1986, or, in the other direction, 2016. Raul and Sylvia may be assimilating, but, the film asks, into what, and when, exactly? As if to continue that question, in the next scene, Raul, a Mexican immigrant, orders two Chinese-chicken salads at an American restaurant whose décor has no definable theme other than a general nostalgia (the mise-en-scène includes a carousel horse, a sombrero, and older wooden tennis rackets), a moment not so much critical as genuinely perplexed by the circumstances one often encounters within a no-space, no-time global economy, manifest here in the mundane context of a husband and wife on a date (figure 13).

But while this film might appeal to left-leaning progressives, if not Marxists or others who would dismantle the system, *Fast Food Nation* does not seek to replace global capitalism or democracy; in this respect, it is quite the opposite of *The Jungle*, where Sinclair advocates socialism directly, though the absence in the film of the book's specific, programmatic ending, which lays out ideas for reform, leaves the issue of larger systemic changes more open-ended. Still, *Nation*, in both film and text form, has concrete and immediate problems it wants to raise awareness of: the contamination of meat; the way cattle are fed; dangerous, even life-threatening factory conditions; the exploitation of immigrants; and

Figure 13. *Fast Food Nation*: vaguely nostalgic mise-en-scène on Sylvia and Raul's date.

other related subjects. In addressing these concerns, *Nation* rethinks a focus on an ever-accelerating present-ness to convey a sense of slowing down, whether at the meatpacking plant or the boardroom, or in the act of simply asking questions and beginning to think. That is not to say the film eschews a sense of real urgency in the need to address these issues, but it does leave open the possibility that engaging socially as an individual can be a process of discovery that need not be arrived at as quickly as a value meal's preparation. Amber's story represents this desire to engage; Linklater has remarked how autobiographical Amber's character is, both in her relatively insular life within Cody and in the importance of a figure—here, as with Linklater, an uncle—whose mere presence conveys an expanded sense of politics, culture, and the possibilities of life itself (Robey 27). During the night out with Uncle Pete, which begins with some gentle taboo breaking, as they visit a local bar, Amber reveals that she wants to be an astronaut, an aspiration the film never smirks at. Likewise, the film never views Uncle Pete's own idealism with irony either, his discussions of following one's passions and listening to oneself above all else congruent with so many other similar moments in Linklater's other work (one could almost imagine that this is Jesse, visiting Cody, between trips to Europe). This becomes the catalyst for Amber's gradual awakening, as she attends a college party, becomes fascinated with the politics they discuss, joins an activist group, authors a plan to free cows, and experiences a letdown when the plan fails. But even as she exhorts the cattle to leave, the film never condescends; it may allow for humor, but it is not a humor at Amber's expense so much as it is about the levity of a genuine political act that was ill-planned. Amber may be frustrated by the night's events, but the experience, much like her quitting the job at Mickey's, points to something she is beginning to think about more seriously: her present circumstances and a future to which these actions might contribute. Schlosser closes his text with a related gesture, as he envisions "future historians" who might "consider the American fast food industry a relic of the twentieth century" and surprisingly, given the journey we have taken, ends by saying, "Despite all evidence to the contrary, I remain optimistic" (288). Although the film closes on a more downbeat note, with Don's concessions and a near-endless supply of assembly-line burgers, it too seems to retain an essential optimism, largely through Amber but also in its respect for the dignity of all of its characters. In so doing, it asks us to see those seemingly immutable lights on our landscape, or at least the problems that underlie the business practices that keep many of them lit, as just as capable of change, and just as finite, as we ourselves are.

Fields of Play and Waiting for Orson

Writing to his friend Benjamin Bailey in 1817, poet John Keats reflected on the subject of happiness, "I look not for it if it be not in the present hour—nothing startles me beyond the Moment. The setting sun will always set me to rights—or if a Sparrow come before my Window I take part in its existence [*sic*] and pick about the Gravel" (1208). Much of this volume's interest in the present moment, as articulated in these films, is undoubtedly indebted to the rich cultural and aesthetic heritage of Romanticism that Keats helped to shape. Romanticism, as the introduction to this book indicates, has more generally fallen out of favor in cinema studies. But in the case of Linklater's work, the lingering influence of Romanticism seems apt, given that the films draw so heavily not only on the richness of the present moment but also on other ideas we associate with this tradition, including the valorization of personal intuition over appeals to convention, the admiration for both expertise and amateurism, the inherent power of creative acts to unlock previously untapped possibilities, and the fascination for those who either reject the system outright or continually drift away from it, in spite of themselves. Beyond these aspects, the films place a very high regard on passion itself, in whatever form it takes—an idea Linklater has discussed explicitly, as in the interview that appears here—and this subject is central to the last two films of this volume, embodied in their primary figures: Augie Garrido, the highly successful University of Texas baseball coach, in *Inning by Inning: A Portrait of a Coach,* and Orson Welles, the focus of the protagonist's adulation and eventual disappointment, in *Me and Orson Welles* (a film where Welles is only one of many, including the protagonist, who seek out experiences driven by passion). *Inning,* a documentary, returned Linklater to the genre he had explored with *Live from Shiva's Dance Floor,* if not also the nonfiction leanings of some feature films such as *Slacker* and *Waking Life.* Here, however, the process required exponentially more time than *Shiva,* and unlike those other films, it had even less of a "road map" at its outset, since neither Linklater nor producer Brian Franklin could anticipate how the team would compete during the course of the 2006 season, the film's initial focus. Shooting both practices and games, Franklin followed the players and coaches over a few months, as Linklater set about interviewing journalists, former players, former assistants, family members, friends, admirers of Garrido, and Garrido himself. (The project shifted to a portrait model, rather than one driven by the race to a championship, after the team did not perform as they had in years prior.) After this Linklater and Adair spent an additional eighteen months editing the footage into an affectionate tribute to Garrido's life and career, and although an Austin premiere took place at the Paramount Theatre, its main domestic distribution occurred on the ESPN cable-television station on June 15, 2008, one of the first days of the College World Series and also, not coincidentally, Father's Day (DeFore). Drawing on Linklater's investment in baseball and friendship with the coach, the film attempts to give viewers a sense of Garrido's daily interactions with players and his larger educational ethos, where failure instructs, even if winning is preferred.

Inning by Inning: A Portrait of a Coach raises an important question, however, almost immediately: is it a film? In many respects, the way one answers the question is less interesting than how it demonstrates a loosening of the term, a well-acknowledged observation that is nonetheless worth exploring here for a moment. *Film,* in its current state, no longer designates a single medium, with digital formats existing alongside (and sometimes replacing) celluloid, and it likewise connotes a theatrical experience much less than it once did, with the proliferation of alternative reception contexts. In its more common usage, *film* often simply conveys a general running time—anywhere from ninety minutes to three hours, though usually in the two-hour range—as well as the promise of a "whole" experience, completing narratives or arguments rather than serializing them into multiple parts, notwithstanding sequels or series of films that use the same characters. *Film* also sometimes connotes aesthetic seriousness, an aspect ESPN Films, the division of ESPN that financed *Inning,* has relied upon in many of its offerings, including, for example, the 30 for 30 series, which, like *Inning,* uses recognizable film directors to produce even more cache. Of course, the idea of *film* being additive to television belies how central television has already become for most contemporary cinema reception. Barbara Klinger has observed, "Although the Internet is developing as a place to screen films, television remains at the center of the domestic film universe. Presently, TV is not only the most important post-theatrical exhibition site for films; it also constitutes a fundamental screen experience for film viewers" (7). Even more succinctly, John T. Caldwell has noted, "Cinema, in some odd ways, has become television" (96), a statement not unrelated to television's own changes in the post-network era, where channels have become more specialized, so that a station devoted entirely to films, or sports, or food, or game shows might thrive, even multiply, as ESPN has done, with its many channels both on television and online. *Inning by Inning* reflects this context in its specialized focus: it dispenses with explanations about the rules or larger histories that might be useful for a novice, such as the structure of the College World Series or the development of NCAA athletics in the twentieth century. Instead, *Inning* assumes a knowledge of and love for, or at least an appreciation for why one might develop a knowledge of and love for, the sport at its center: baseball.

To return to some of the issues outlined at the outset, perhaps no game in U.S. athletic history has more romantic associations than baseball, and cinema has contributed in no small part to that. As S. W. Pope has noted, "To this day, baseball's preferred ideology runs untrammeled throughout the nation's cultural landscape. Journalists, popular intellectuals, and filmmakers continue to stoke the flames of baseball's 'innocent,' mythical past," citing *Field of Dreams* (1989), *The Babe* (1992), and *A League of Their Own* (1992) as examples (80). *Inning* invokes this history in part through its return, again and again, to the idea of joy within the game, and even more so through some early commentary from Kevin Costner, a Cal State–Fullerton alumnus and friend of Garrido whose appearance cannot help but recall his roles as a current or former baseball player (*Bull Durham* [1988], *For the Love of the Game* [1999], and *The Upside of Anger* [2005]) or inspired fan (*Field of Dreams*) that also link the film to that "mythical past." The style of the film, too, brings to mind the most famous of the sport's documentaries on television (and one Pope critiques as well), Ken Burns's PBS series *Baseball* (1994), updated in 2010 with the two-part *The Tenth Inning*. Unlike *Baseball*, *Inning* eschews voice-over, instead relying on the voices of its participants and occasional captions to relay expository information. But the talking-head interviews, blending oral history with still photography and often panning over the image in a technique Burns popularized, show its debt to that series. Moreover, the focus on a single person's achievements also aligns it with what Tom Robson has taken baseball films to task for: that is, an overemphasis on the individual over the community. "By prioritizing the single man over the collective," Robson writes, "these films connect to the inherently individualistic ethos of U.S. life, and baseball serves as a supremely appropriate vehicle to construct, support, and propagate this ideology of individualism" (1). In many ways, viewers of *Inning* will not find much to overturn either Pope's or Robson's hypotheses, given that it rarely, if ever, critiques the game or offers other perspectives that might present a more complex figure at its center. It similarly never gets into the extraordinary revenues that college sports generate and the increasingly close relationships among corporate sponsors and university athletics. But these are ultimately subjects for another film; *Inning*'s primary purpose is to celebrate a life that has meant a great deal to many, many people, including its director. It is a portrait of love, and although the tone might at times invite unhealthy nostalgic reveries, we should not discount the importance of love or passion itself, both in general and, more specifically, in this portrayal of Garrido or the debts that so many players articulate when they talk about his guidance. (In this way, although focused on an individual, one senses the collective in those who have won and lost with him over his now several decades of coaching.)

To construct its portrait, *Inning* alternates between sections based loosely around a subject, such as the importance of fundamentals or the experience of failure, and a rough chronology that presents Garrido's early life and career before focusing almost exclusively, in the last half of the film, on his teams' five national championships, beginning with Cal State–Fullerton in 1979 and continuing through the University of Texas's 2005 victory, which effectively serves as the end, save a few final comments from Garrido and others. Montages of the players in action, whether in a game or not, underscore the larger sense that the team is always striving to be better and that Garrido's presence imbues the program with a work ethic that is also one of play. For example, a practice montage, early in the film, is accompanied by an upbeat guitar melody; brief shots of players fielding a ground ball or bunting in a batting cage show dedication, but the music underscores these activities as ultimately fun, even when the players themselves may be hard at work. Here, another important aspect of the film becomes apparent: its heavy and quite literal reliance on Garrido's voice (often as a kind of de facto narrator). Interviews with him outnumber those with others, and he is frequently the main speaker in any given interaction with players, whether counseling individually or emphatically addressing a locker room after a win or a loss. In this same scene, for instance, although the first speaker is Cliff Hatter, Cal State–Fullerton's head equipment manager, Garrido soon takes over, in an interview, as he talks about his borrowings from other sports—football and basketball—to animate his practices, before the film transitions into another moment of Garrido's speaking, this time at an actual practice, where he makes an analogy of playing pool to illustrate a point about pitching. Another important technique of this scene, and the film more generally, is the way that Garrido's voice is audible even when his face is not visible, a familiar documentary convention that allows his reflections to saturate the film even further, so that he will begin speaking before we actually see him and continue even after his image has left the screen. In this way, even when he is not expressly in the shot, Garrido's presence inflects nearly every moment in the film, its digressive, organic transitions aided by this frequently recurring aural accompaniment. But though these and other aspects emphasize that presence, they do so, paradoxically, to underscore a quality the film places a high premium on: that is, the coach's essential selflessness when it comes to educating his players. The film constantly returns to this idea, as it does when Bill Kernan notes that the greatest contribution Garrido makes is to give players "themselves"; for all of its emphasis on Garrido, the film also looks outward toward the players he has attempted to prepare both for the remainder of a season and for the lives that follow the sport, whether after a long professional career or immediately following the last game of a senior year.

In this book's interview, Linklater remarks that the film is a portrait of himself "to a degree" (in the same way that, as he notes, Bennett Miller's film about Speed Levitch, *The Cruise,* is also about Miller). *Inning* bears this out in several ways. For one, Garrido discusses his decision as a young person to depart from the work his parents and others, including a high school guidance counselor, said he was capable of, much as Linklater, too, has characterized his early biography by a strong internal compass and a disdain for the advice of authority figures when it came to determining life choices. One sees this in the films, as in *Before Sunrise,* when Jesse talks about the directives his parents and others once gave him, telling Celine, "By the time I was in high school, I was dead set on listening to what everybody thought I should be doing with my life and just kind of doing the opposite," confessing that he "could never get very excited about other people's ambitions for my life." Other ideas that *Inning* explores reflect Linklater as much as Garrido, including the long view toward failure as instructive or the sense that learning is a lifelong, ongoing process. In terms of this text's focus, the very title of the documentary, *Inning by Inning,* reflects an investment in a present temporality, even if the emphasis on preparation implies a future performance—and even if such preparation often stems from the lessons of the past. Unlike some of the other films investigated thus far, however, *Inning* is less about temporal experience more generally and more about the clarity achieved in parsing a larger competitive experience down to its most essential moment—within every inning, if not every swing of the bat. Late in the film, Garrido articulates this idea explicitly: "The goal at the University of Texas is to win the national championship. Well, you can't do that. It's too far away . . . so you have to come back to more immediate goals, and immediate goals keep you in the moment. So that's why we break the game down from pitch to pitch." Viewers familiar with Linklater's other films might find themselves recalling Mitch on the mound in *Dazed and Confused,* where he only needs a last out to win the game, even if victory will immediately doom him to the seniors calling from the stands. In the scene, the slow-motion cinematography and cessation of sound are familiar stylistic tropes of the athlete in total concentration, and *Dazed* relies on them to convey the same essential philosophy we find Garrido speaking about, more than a decade later: the sense that a game, whether Little League or professional, can be won only a single pitch (or hit) at a time. The film illustrates this attitude at many points, such as a brief scene where Garrido speaks to a player during a game; in the shot, Garrido faces away from the camera as he counsels his pitcher, "I want you to have fun with . . . all that you have left of this game, and this is a chance for you to show your character and your courage." With the competition still underway, the film demonstrates how precarious the line between a win and loss can be—how a subtle shift, in the moment, might make the difference. Also, the style of the scene, with the camera operator placed awkwardly behind and away from Garrido, presumably so as not to be intrusive, accentuates the unpredictable aspects of the game even further through the more improvised setup (figure 14). None of Garrido's more supportive moments, however, should indicate an indifference to losing, as an impassioned address to the 2006 team attests, when he delivers an expletive-laden speech about the loss they just experienced. A caption tells us, "Texas won their next 10 games and the Big 12 Conference Championship," implying a calculation to the outrage, or, at least, that his methods include a wider range than the even-keeled advice we have seen him provide elsewhere. But whether we find Garrido angry, as in this heated outburst, or, as is most often the case, reflective, even buoyant, the film pays tribute to its central figure for his educational skills, his knowledge of the game, and his charming, infectious demeanor. Above all, *Inning by Inning* celebrates his passion and passion more generally, particularly in the sense that one can always start anew—for a coach, when a season opens; for a filmmaker, when a new project comes to life; and, as in the next feature, for anyone involved

Figure 14. The camera positioned behind Garrido as he coaches a pitcher in *Inning by Inning*.

in theater, when the house lights dim, the curtains rise, and the first actor begins to speak.

Originally a 2003 novel by Robert Kaplow, *Me and Orson Welles* follows a week in the life of Richard Samuels, a fictional adolescent whose impromptu audition lands him a small part in one of American theater's most famous runs, the 1937 staging of *Julius Caesar* as fascist allegory, in the very first production of Orson Welles and John Houseman's newly formed Mercury Theatre. Kaplow, a high school teacher and young-adult novelist, was inspired by a photograph in an old *Theatre Arts Monthly,* where Lucius, played by a boy whom Richard was loosely based upon, serenades Brutus, played by Welles himself, in an image the film reproduces almost exactly (Warnet). Screenwriters Holly Gent Palmo and Vince Palmo found *Me and Orson Welles* in an Austin bookstore and, deciding it would make a good film, passed it along to Linklater, who agreed, securing rights to the project in late 2006. From there the Palmos would write the script, with Linklater consulting Kaplow the following spring. Then, in the summer of 2007, Kaplow alerted Linklater to an off-Broadway production of a play called *Rosebud: The Lives of Orson Welles;* the play starred the relatively unknown Christian McKay, who met with Linklater and was cast shortly thereafter. Once McKay was set, other casting would follow, including Zac Efron, a young actor most famous as Troy in the Disney *High School Musical* franchise, for Richard; Claire Danes, for Sonja; and other talented performers, for the rest of the Mercury troupe and Richard's acquaintances and family. Shooting took place in the spring of 2008, in the Isle of Man, London, and New York; the Isle of Man's Gaiety Theatre provided the crucial interior of the Mercury, a location also motivated by the project's financial backing, CinemaNX, a company funded by the Isle of Man to attract film production (Dawtrey, "CinemaNX Boards Trio"). Although the film, once completed, would screen at the Toronto International Film Festival in September, it did not find a distributor, somewhat surprisingly, given Efron's popularity and presumed bankability. The lack of interest, however, reflected serious changes across the industry. Major studios had reduced or phased out many specialty divisions, such as New Line or Warner Independent, that might have supported *Welles* in the past (Dawtrey, "European Film Sales"), and no other companies were willing to fill that vacuum, particularly as the grueling economic events of the year unfolded and the United States found itself in a deep recession. Eventually, through an unusual distribution arrangement composed of several companies (CinemaNX, Freestyle, and others) (Kay), the film opened on November 25, 2009, in the United States, and appeared on DVD the following summer, again through an unusual arrangement, an exclusive deal with the Target chain in the United States (and Tesco in the UK). Whether this brief history prefigures bleaker days ahead for certain kinds of cinema or, alternatively, simply signals a shift, small or seismic, that will necessarily have benefits and drawbacks has yet to be clear. Such anxieties are perhaps heightened when set against this narrative's own, the first production of a new theater already deep into debt and unable to recover should the play prove unsuccessful. But while the film's production history may bring these economic facts into focus, they are hardly the central concern of *Me and Orson Welles;* if anything, George Coulouris's dour advice to "polish thy résumé" or other comments that the production might fail serve only to confirm Richard's sense, as well as the film's, that the Mercury teems with life and exuberance, within the naive dream space of a cinematic, near magical New York City.

So much of the film centers on Manhattan, as filtered through Richard's reverie; while much of the novel takes place there, the film goes even further by shortening scenes and cutting characters associated with school and home. (Of the roughly 105 minutes of narrative time, less than 5 take place outside the city.) Furthermore, a transitional motif underscores this urban elation: whenever the film leaves Manhattan, it returns by means of a rapidly moving tracking shot, usually following Richard's walk through the streets, as an upbeat jazz score accompanies his stride. This portrayal of New York draws on its long mythology as wellspring of twentieth-century culture—a romantic vision, to be sure, but one often shared by the period's own chroniclers. Hallie Flanagan, head of the Federal Theatre Project who wrote of those years in *Arena,* describes "the burning centripetal force of New York City" that "attracted as one particle of its whirling life, theatre talent" and "transmuted that talent into the sharply gleaming, hard-faceted New York stage" (51). Likewise, theater critic Edith J. R. Isaacs, in the January 1938 *Theatre Arts Monthly* (which also includes the image of Lucius and Brutus), marvels at the offerings on Broadway in late 1937—noting, in particular, Clifford Odets's *Golden Boy* and an adaptation of John Steinbeck's *Of Mice and Men*—as she describes "the wave of pleasurable excitement" that greeted these and other important performances that closed the year, including the Mercury's *Caesar* (11). The film taps into this vibrant history also at the level of casting, with Gretta Adler, played by Zoe Kazan; not only does her character name reference one of the more famous members of the 1930s Group Theatre, Stella Adler, but she is the granddaughter of another of the Group Theatre's most famous members, Elia Kazan. Beyond theater, the film's soundtrack, too, with its near-constant presence of period-era jazz, as in an instrumental "They Can't Take That Away from Me" while Richard pores over the mementos of his one and only performance, characterizes the city as music mecca, seen also in Richard's browsing through sheet music at the piano store where he first meets Gretta, mourning the passing of Gershwin. The presence of radio in various scenes, along with the numerous newspapers and magazines that show up either in clippings or being read aloud by Welles, also places New York at the center of the rapid media expansion of the period, and the mixture of references to high culture, as in the visits to the Metropolitan Museum of Art, and popular culture, as in a subplot involving Selznick's casting of *Gone with the Wind* (1939), suggests that at least part of Manhattan's cosmopolitanism lies in its relaxing of such aesthetic distinctions, an attitude Welles embodies in shifting effortlessly between Shakespeare and *The Late Addition for Love*. The city's rich cultural life, in short, is everywhere on display, an aspect increased exponentially by Richard's awakening desire to participate in it, in whatever way he might. When he later tells Gretta, "I just want to be a part of it all," naming several different creative activities he might pursue, including "acting, writing, music, plays" (a list that repeats a similar exchange with Sonja, when she asks him, "What do you love?"), his enthusiasm for the arts seems to grow organically out of simply being in this place. In the film's New York, it seems possible that an upstart's singing of a Wheaties jingle might lead to a night onstage with Orson Welles, and our familiarity with the basic premise, drawing as it does on those of classical Hollywood and later, also enables the implausible narrative's completion, Richard's rise no more unlikely than Kathy's, for example, from Coconut Grove girl to A-list star of Monumental Pictures in *Singin' in the Rain* (1952).

Part of what makes this narrative even more alluring is the promise of much historical fiction, which is a sense of imaginary proximity, often justifiably critiqued, in relation to people and events long past. Unlike *The Newton Boys,* however, whom most viewers would likely know little about prior to seeing the film, Welles's iconicity is so strong that it becomes the means by which the film convinces us that *this is Welles himself.* Much of the impetus in this regard is achieved simply through casting, with McKay's physical likeness, vocal inflections, and gestures calling up the young Charles Foster Kane, strutting about the offices of the *Inquirer* long before his retreat to Xanadu, among other images of Welles gleaned from previously encountered films, photographs, and other texts. In her *New York Times* review of McKay's *Rosebud* performance, Ginia Bellafante remarks, "What nature hasn't already bestowed on him in Wellesian aura and appearance, he meticulously affects. The jowls, the quizzical eyes and sonorous baritone: Mr. McKay is Welles to the soles of his feet, annunciating [*sic*] every word as if the future of proper diction depended on him." And just as our own sense of Welles relies upon a pastiche of varied, even conflicting sources, the film too insists there is not a single Welles but many, an idea that fits the one he himself cultivated, in his often inscrutable characters, none more famous than Kane, or in his own self-making with journalists (as Simon Callow notes, "He publicly constructed himself . . . in a medium that he courted and denounced in equal measure" [xv]). Peter Conrad's *Orson Welles: The Stories of His Life* explicitly builds an investigation around a many-faceted Welles, his first chapter entitled "So Many of Me," and James Naremore ends his *The Magic World of Orson Welles* by noting how "the scholarly attempt to define or restore Welles's works is . . . like Thompson's search for Rosebud," where "a missing piece might complete a puzzle" but "even when the piece is found it cannot sum up the story" (276). These attitudes inform the multiple Orsons we encounter here. There is Orson the genius, a talent so immense he need not prepare to achieve greatness, as in his CBS Radio appearance, where a gliding Steadicam trails in his wake, as he woos a young woman, later spontaneously interpolating lines from Booth Tarkington into a performance the other actors can only envy. There is Orson the infant, who demands immediate satisfaction of his cravings—for food, as in the steaks and pineapple juice he consumes, or sex, as in his multiple trysts, such as the night with Sonja, one of the film's darkest moments, both in its brief acknowledgment of the sexual politics of the period as well as in Sonja's casual acceptance of them that seems both liberating and tragic at once. There are other Orsons, too: a tyrannical Orson, who tells the cast and crew, "I own the store!"; a gracious Orson, telling the same group, moments later, "You're a magnificent company on par with any theatrical company in the world"; a contrarian Orson, arguing with Houseman at every turn; a lazy Orson, who will not rehearse; an industrious Orson, who rehearses too much; and others, including a cowardly Orson, who allows Joe Cotton to tell Richard that he has been fired. At two junctures, the film even seems to present a confessional Orson: once, when riding in the ambulance with Richard, Welles recalls the untimely deaths of his mother and father, and later, in Bryant Park, when convincing Richard to return to the play, Welles tells him, "You see, if I can be Brutus for ninety minutes tonight—I mean really be him, from the inside out—then for ninety minutes, I get this miraculous reprieve from being myself," the camera's slow push-in underscoring this more exposed version of Welles. But the film's cumulative effect suggests that even these exchanges may reflect other personae, interchangeable as he sees fit (as does, regarding the moment in Bryant Park, a similar speech Welles gives to calm Coulouris's stage fright). When Houseman declares, after an abysmal preview, "This is the essential Orson Welles moment, isn't it?" the film has already made it clear that *every* moment is essential, or none of them are, since no one is more or less "Welles" than the others. They are all *him,* as we might imagine his being, and here lies a subtle comparison between his multiple personae and the compositing process one must adopt when imagining him, weighing various sources, performances, and references against one another (or allowing for the paradoxes to exist, side by side). That said, part of this process may involve resisting certain versions of Welles we encounter here, as James Naremore reminds us, noting how poorly this Welles treats the embattled Samuel Leve. For Naremore, much of this stems from the original novel, where Welles makes an anti-Semitic remark as he calls Leve (in a moment only Richard overhears) a "credit-stealing, son-of-a-bitch Jew." When Richard confronts him on the remark, Welles responds again, "I called him a credit-stealing, son-of-a-bitch Jew because that's exactly what he is" (Kaplow 173). These exchanges are struck from the film, but even the antagonism that remains in the adaptation seems overwrought, Naremore argues. As he writes, "In Welles's defense, I can only say that his quite lengthy and courageous fight against racial prejudice is a matter of public record" ("Films of the Year, 2009" 30); he also disputes the implication that Welles had little to do with the stage designs—countermanded by Houseman's memoir—as well as the film's portrayal of "the politics of the Mercury" (31) and the enactment of the play itself (though he finds much to like in the film more generally, including it, as he did, on his "best of" list for 2009). Still, despite these critiques and potentially others one might make with regard to the general history or Welles in particular, the film relies on an innate sense of excitement at the possibility of rediscovering, if not reanimating, images of Orson Welles, even if issues such as those Naremore raises wisely remind us of the limitations in any such experience.

Other "rediscoveries" accompany that of Welles—the Mercury is held up as a site of historical-fiction fascination, its trapdoors and multiple levels an extension of its director's unfathomable personality, while also functioning as an early archive of at least one Wellesian artifact through which Richard, and we, encounter him: in its office, an image from *Doctor Faustus* and an advertisement for ham—as in "ham actor"—jokingly taped over it. At times, the film stokes historical interest in the Mercury as the site of *Julius Caesar*, largely through the final performance, in a theater buff's dream of re-creation: here are the famous "Nuremburg lights" illuminating the stage; here are the long, dark trench coats; here is Caesar, stumbling down the row of conspirators, knives gleaming; and here is the famous murder of Cinna, walls awash in red as the mob scatters, leaving the audience gasping as the poet vanishes. Beyond this one night in November 1937, the Mercury also serves to connect Richard, and us, to a longer fabric of theater history that goes back to Shakespeare and beyond, not only through Welles's interest in a fidelity to Elizabethan language, if not always staging, but also in smaller moments, notably when Richard holds a match up to the ceiling, seeing "Consequences, 1914" with the name "Horace Braham" written there, a reference to a production and actor in the Mercury building's former occupant, the Comedy Theatre. But while these and other pleasures of historical fiction are prominent, the film, too, explores something very close to the heart of this book's interests: that is, the temporality of a theater rehearsal, sometimes characterized by action but, at the same time, by inaction, one hour becoming several as afternoon moves to evening and into tomorrow. When Norman Lloyd, in one of the first rehearsal scenes, advises Richard, "Oh, kid, you'll soon realize the principal occupation of the Mercury Theatre is waiting for Orson," he hits on this subject directly, and one might even think of the film as an ode to waiting—nowhere near as extreme as *It's Impossible to Learn to Plow by Reading Books,* but still lovingly paying tribute to the activity that most theater actors, technicians, and even directors do quite a lot of, and that is to simply sit in the rehearsal space—in this case, the theater itself—and wait, watching other people run through their lines, move sets to a new place, move them back, stand around, and exist in a temporality characterized by a strange mixture of hurry and delay, industry and sloth. It is not as though nothing happens during rehearsals—the first rehearsal, for example, sets up and builds upon several narrative threads: Richard's budding romance with Sonja, Norman's comic persona, Norman's concern about the Cinna scene, Houseman's financial anxieties, Welles's affairs and marriage, Sam Leve's concerns about the program, Welles and Coulouris's working relationship, and Welles's treatment of Richard with both condescension and affirmation. All the while, however, what much of the people do as the long scene unfolds is sit and wait. One player smokes and chuckles while Welles thunders on about a thespian rival's *Time* cover story (figure 15); others also sit idly, illustrating that sense of the rehearsal's time as almost con-

Figure 15. Rehearsals in *Me and Orson Welles*: as Welles talks, actors smoke and wait.

templative, in moments, but moving to a high-energy pace in an instant, when Welles demands it. Such idleness and activity occur at the margins of almost all of the rehearsals, where Richard and others are frequently shot as they rest in the mostly empty audience seats; although this allows for some clever blocking, where conversations might be filmed with all participants in the same shot (since they are facing the same direction), it also indicates the way time stretches in rehearsals, as one waits to be called upon, but very often just waits. For Richard, such waiting is full of promise, a time of the present moment when, despite the inconsistency of the process, he does indeed seem to be learning about the stage, so that when he finally performs on opening night, he performs well, a payoff both ironic, since his rehearsals are usually cut short by Welles, and sincere, since that waiting process of theatrical absorption seems to have meant something. When Richard finds out he has been fired, Joe Cotton tells him, "You go home, kid," to which he responds, "This is home," standing in the mostly empty theater, a mourning of his time at the Mercury, certainly, but equally of the rehearsal process. In *Me and Orson Welles,* waiting in a theater is its own reward, one not unrelated to Gretta's activity in the museum, where she, too, waits, contemplating the urn, in a gesture that returns us to Romanticism and the passion for passion itself. When Richard and Gretta leave the museum at film's end, they both mention "possibilities"—a joke about Gretta's creative-writing instructor, but equally an embrace of the arts and the present moment within which these two characters might explore them, whether in a rehearsal space or, now, within a cinematic New York indeed rich with possibilities. The Keatsian urn is an appropriate site for the final scene, given how this and so many of the attitudes in this film, if not Linklater's work more generally, draw on the Romantic tradition, even as they sometimes acknowledge its limits and reject any one overly rigid interpretive framework, a Romantic disposition in itself.

The sense of time and the present moment that I have sketched out in this book is one of many paths through Linklater's filmography, and as the introduction indicates, my hope is that it will start, rather than foreclose, further conversations on his work. Like films, books are temporal objects, and this one's readings will change in the future, simply by being encountered in another time. More pragmatically, its ending can speak only provisionally on what will follow. As of this writing, Linklater is editing *Bernie,* and he also has future projects in the works, including a fascinating project filmed with the same actors over a twelve-year span (they have completed nine) that will narrate the history of a fictional boy as the actors age in real time, a cinematic experiment close to that of the *Before* films and continuing his dialogue with cinema and time. To step back a bit from Linklater's work and consider film and writing more broadly, perhaps the future of cinema and the future of the book are on similar paths, as new media open new doors, and new problems, for storing and creating knowledge in both. Scholar Jerome McGann, in a suggestive passage from *Radiant Textuality,* describes how one might, in looking up at the stars at night, remember that "your eyes are taking but a snapshot of an eons-old cosmic event in which you and your camera are engulfed and borne along," to illustrate a kind of "quantum effect" that might inform the way writers produce criticism, a methodology that would be capable of "grasping the objective instability of the subjects of our study . . ., of our tools, and of the results . . . generated through the study processes" (163–64). Regardless of where cinema, the book, writing, and new media may be heading, and regardless of the ways that such instabilities might be enabling or limiting, my hope is that, like so many of the characters who inhabit these films, we continue to take the notions of intellectual curiosity and humanities-based inquiry seriously, the objects that we read, watch, study, discuss, argue over, or think about able to teach us something new, over and over again, provided we are willing to give them the time.

Interview with Richard Linklater |

This interview took place in two phone conversations on November 30 and December 8, 2010, when Linklater spoke to me from his Detour office in Austin, Texas, while on postproduction for *Bernie*. Because we covered his entire filmography, our conversations generated more dialogue than would be possible to print. As a result, I have condensed and excised certain passages. I have also edited many of the false starts, repetitions, and pauses in speech that are a part of everyday conversation but are distracting on the page, and I have moved one section to account for his going back to add to an answer on an earlier question. That said, what follows are Linklater's own words on his films and related subjects.

DAVID JOHNSON: You've talked in the past [about college] being a time when you started getting interested in literature, in theater, in film, and so forth. Were there any particular experiences around that time that turned you on to that, or was it just a general disposition to being open to those sorts of things?

RICHARD LINKLATER: You know, I had always been a reader, but in the school system I grew up in, it felt like a small part of the big experience. In high school I wanted to grow up and be a novelist of some kind, that's what I was thinking—I wanted to write or express myself, I knew that at an early age. But . . . the great thing about college for me was to have that go up a notch, where suddenly I'm in English classes, and there's a professor, and he makes a living talking about that. And then all of the students, they don't care about sports—that wasn't the emphasis. The emphasis was these great books; we're talking about Kafka, we're talking about Dostoevsky. To have that kind of excitement, and to feel like that was sanctioned—it wasn't just a little subdivision, a little asterisk of your life, it was like, wow, it can be front and center, you can be an English major. Then, through that, I took a playwriting class that was, while technically in the English Department—this is my sophomore year—a lot of drama majors, and I met a lot of people in the Drama Department. I think the summer before I had started dating a girl who was in the Drama Department, an actress, and I remember going to a couple of productions she was in, then meeting her friends, and that whole world opened up. It just seemed exciting.

Taking a playwriting class was very different than taking an acting or directing class. Playwriting was a good foot in the door for me, just to study playwrights. And that's when I could feel my ambitions shifting from literature to drama; my new heroes were Edward Albee, Eugene O'Neill, and Sam Shepard. I thought, maybe I'm a playwright. I wrote a few plays. I really enjoyed it, and that's where I was going, just for a semester, but it has fueled my lifelong love of theater ever since—the romance of it, the atmosphere of it. But then, somewhere in there, right on the heels of that, was watching movies. That was the early days of the VCR—no one had them at home yet, this is like '81—but in the English Department there was one. And I noticed there was this little film [group]. [I'd get] a couple of friends, and we'd go watch the movie. The professor—every English professor is a film critic, right?—was Ralph Pease, who was a real film buff. And so we sat there and would talk about the movie after. I really enjoyed that. And that was just enough to get me started with movies.

Shortly thereafter, I was done with school, and I was working offshore in Houston, but in my time off, I started looking up movies, and that was still the heyday of repertory cinema. That's when I found myself in the theater all of the time; I would watch four movies a day. That's where that started. And a few people I knew were doing theater in Houston, so I would go to a play or something. But for the most part, I just found myself at the movies. So all of that is a pretty quick little segue, from literature to theater to film, in six months.

DJ: And when did you find yourself getting drawn to Austin? When did you make that move?

RL: You know, Austin is the kind of place you think about, if you grow up in Texas. It's the cool city where I'd had friends who'd gone to college—you come visit, and there's live music and all this stuff going on, so it was always in the back of my mind . . . but it was about a year, a year and a half into my Houston offshore time, [that] a collection of shorts [screened] that had been made in Austin, in and around the university. Some were university, and some weren't. They were really interesting. The two highlights of that for me was one called *Speed of Light* by Brian Hansen and another called *Invasion of the Aluminum People* by David Boone. Unfortunately, both of those guys died young. I never got to know them. Jonathan Demme had put together a program of films he had seen in Texas, and he showed them at the Collective for Living Cinema in New York. They played in a little place in Houston, so I went one night and saw those films and thought, "There's filmmaking going on in Austin." I was seguing from thinking I was just going to write to [thinking] I could make films. You know, I had short stories I had written I had adapted to scripts, and I could see the film in my head. I was waking up to the idea that I had this visual ability—I could see the film. So I slowly started to study the technical aspects of filmmaking, in addition to reading everything, the history and stuff. My intensive film history/personal history study segued into film technique and the basics of filmmaking—it was all fun.

DJ: And you make *It's Impossible to Learn to Plow by Reading Books.* Can you tell me a little bit about the genesis of that film—how you started thinking about it and that sort of thing?

RL: Well, I'll call that the several-year culmination, let's say a four-year culmination, of my own little private film school—buying film equipment, shooting a bunch of shorts. You know, I always thought it was funny, with my first film anyone saw, *Slacker.* They acted like it was the first time I had picked up a camera, and I was like, "No, no, no, I have been doing this for a while. You don't want to see any of these films, [but] I've actually very methodically shot many, many, many thousands of feet of film, with many hours of editing." You can't believe how hard I worked doing something that absolutely no other human cared about, all those years. And *Plow* was sort of my graduate thesis film for that little section of my life. . . .

DJ: Right around this time, too, you'd already founded the Austin Film Society, and you were holding screenings. How did all of that feed into your work?

RL: It was all part of the same, inspired by the French New Wave, the way Truffaut and Godard said, I could edit an issue of *Cahiers du Cinéma* or make a film, they're kind of the same. And I took that same approach, [which] was, I spend my day now booking movies, making a poster, showing movies, hustling up an audience for a movie—I felt I was serving cinema in some way. . . .

Without too much effort, I went from underground to just above-ground. It's incredible that everything about the film society and *Slacker*—they're one in the same, from underground to official. We opened *Slacker* the same way we showed Film Society films, in the same theater, hustled up an audience. Suddenly, it was our film, myself and everybody who worked on it. We used the same kind of grassroots methods that we did for the film society. That was just an interesting phase in my twenties, a fun period where that kind of potential was harnessed and taken to some other level. For that, I give a lot of credit to my cohorts. You know, *Slacker* would have gone the same way *Plow* did; I didn't have that element of promotional for my own self. I could get out there and fight to the death for a Robert Bresson film, or an Ozu retrospective, or the Tarkovsky film we're showing, or any of that—hustle, hustle, hustle. When it came to my own film, I was shy. But it was my friends, everybody who worked on *Slacker,* they really got excited and pumped that up and maximized that. Left to my own devices, I wouldn't have done anything. . . .

[On *Slacker*] I enjoyed the collaborative nature of it, and being the leader of an artistic troupe, you know, in that regard. But it's a big challenge. You really have to sublimate your ego to get along, particularly in a dynamic when you're not paying anyone; you really have to keep the ball spinning and make sure everybody's happy. You couldn't be a tyrant or anything. I enjoyed the professionalism of *Dazed,* stepping up to that next level, where it's like, hey, you know what—and that's what I love about the film business—it's competitive, there's a lot of people who want to do it, you're getting paid a decent wage, if you don't like it, or if you're not happy, or if you don't think you have to work very hard, well guess what? There's someone else ready to take your place. Whereas if you're not paying anyone—you know, on *Slacker,* it's like, "Well, my girlfriend's in town, so I'm not going to show up today." What can I say? It's like, "Okay." It was really nice to step up to that professional level [for *Dazed*]. . . .

DJ: [*Dazed*] is the first time you work with Sandra Adair, and you've worked with her so much. Can you talk a little bit about how your collaborative process has evolved?

RL: . . . As we speak, she's in the editing room, and I'm talking to you. I don't have to be over her shoulder. I never did, but I was on those first few movies. Each film I've taken another step back. I remember her telling me, "You can go do something and come back, and I'll show you what I've done." I'm like, "No, no, back it up a couple of frames"—I was just *on her,* because I was like, you're not going to screw up the movie. But over time—well, rather quickly, actually—I've realized that, like any good collaboration, she takes what's there and what you're thinking and makes it a little better. That's what a collaboration is. You take it to some level neither of you could have gotten to.

DJ: That makes me think about a lot of the actors you've worked with over the years, and I'll segue into *Before Sunrise,* because this is when you work with Ethan Hawke and Julie Delpy, and you end up working with them, particularly Hawke, so much. Can you tell me a little bit about how you approach the rehearsal process with actors generally and how you approached the rehearsal process with those two actors in particular?

RL: You know, I love the idea of rehearsing and getting it perfect, and finding new things in rehearsals, so on *Slacker,* that's how I worked—I'd get with the actor and work as much as needed to transform that scene into what it could be, or what it wanted to be. I did that on *Dazed,* also—I entrusted these young actors. I told them, if we do this script word for word, it's going to suck; I need you to bring yourself to this. And we did do the script, but some of the best stuff in it really grew out of the script . . . I really unleashed them. I told them, "Be creative—bring me ideas, let's work on this." It was a great collaboration with each of them. They were all excited, and I think they felt empowered—like, wow, I'm being treated like an artist. Some young actors, it's just, hit your mark, say your line, and look cute. This wasn't that. I really wanted them to be their character. . . . I knew for it to be alive it had to come from them. And to this day, that's how I still work. I just want to empower the actor to feel like they've cocreated this character with me. That potentially works at every level. I found that worked with eleven- and twelve-year-old kids in *School of Rock,* and it works with old actors, too, if they'll allow it to work. . . .

The design of [*Before Sunrise*] was, whoever I cast, I always knew we were going to sit down and rewrite the script again with them. I had even had parts written in the script like, "Café scene, where their relationship goes to a new level of depth and intimacy as they learn more about each other," but I didn't have it. And I said, well, I won't have it until we are into rehearsals for a while and we discover it. Each and every day, it was like, "How are we getting to make this film? How did you get this film financed?" Because we were truly remaking it. I think Martin Shafer at Castle Rock liked the script just enough, a script based on a personal experience of mine . . . [when] I met this woman, we just kind of walked around town, and the whole time I'm thinking, this is the movie. And so eventually I got a friend of mine who was not a screenwriter but an actress in *Slacker*—Kim Krizan. . . . We always had interesting conversations, and I wanted a stronger female presence in the movie. But it's wildly inaccurate to say she wrote—you know, people I've seen [say], well, she wrote the girl part and you wrote the [male part], and it's like, no, no. Kim and I worked on that script for like eleven days, and we had it. That was about a year that that script existed, and got funding, and in the meantime *Dazed and Confused* had come out. Castle Rock wanted to do other films with me, and I showed them that script, and I remember some people had passed on *Before Sunrise* . . . but Martin Shafer goes, "I think that could be good"—bless him, he saw something there. . . . I told him how I worked and wanted to work, and it was just getting the two most creative young people.

So Julie and Ethan were cast—and that's its own long process, everything I mention in two seconds here is its own months-long process, narrowing it down to Julie and Ethan . . . getting them finally in a room together for three weeks and reworking the whole thing was the key. And we worked on weekends; the night before the end, we're still rewriting that scene, so it was just this living, breathing process. But I love that—what you're doing, you want to be alive and to be part of the process, the definition of process oriented. . . .

DJ: After this one, *subUrbia* is the next one released. When did you first see *subUrbia* performed, and when did you first start thinking this might make a good film?

RL: I was in Vienna. I had been a big Eric Bogosian fan—I had seen a few of his things, *Sex, Drugs, Rock and Roll* and a couple of other things, and read some of it, so I was a fan of his. And then Ethan told me about this buddy of his, Steve Zahn—who I had met by then, I had auditioned, actually—who was an actor who was kicking ass in this play, *subUrbia,* and I was like, I can't wait to get back to the U.S. and see that. I remember, it was after we wrapped *Before Sunrise*—so we're talking summer–fall '94—I flew to New York and saw it twice, on a Friday and a Sunday matinee. I remember going to a party—standing up on a rooftop, overlooking the river at a friend's house—and sitting down and thinking, how would that work as a movie? It seemed very cinematic to me, that night after seeing the play. . . . And then, Bogosian had heard I'd come to the play. He called me up, and we started talking, and he told me how much he liked *Dazed.* He said, "You know that guy in the backseat, saying he wants to be a lawyer, you know?"—Adam Goldberg's character—he said, "That wasn't sort of like me, that wasn't kind of like me, that *was* me, that *is* me." [*Laughs.*] So he had grown up in the 'burbs of Woburn, Massachusetts, and we had a lot in common. People always thought we were a strange pairing, but actually Eric and I were a whole lot alike—so much in common about our backgrounds and how we came into the arts, a view of the world, and everything. . . .

And then *subUrbia* happened, when *Newton Boys* got pushed for casting—you know, with studio films, the planets really have to line up perfect. . . . One day we're in preproduction; the next day, the film's on hold. I remember going home that very night and calling up Bogosian and saying, hey, you know *subUrbia*? Maybe we should try to do that, because I felt I was sitting on about a six-month window now. We had talked about it—how quickly could we do it? It just segued right into it, which I was really happy to do. I think people took *subUrbia* lightly, because it came out of nowhere, but it didn't really. I had seen it—at that point, it had been a couple of years—I had thought about it for a long time. Eric and I had talked about it. But then once we really sat down to do it, the adaptation went pretty quickly, just working on it, what to cut, play to film. We shot in twenty-three days, and it all went pretty quick.

DJ: You've talked in the past—particularly in relation to *Fast Food Nation*—about that idea of someone who's a younger person who knows what they don't want to do, economically or socially. I'm thinking of Jeff in *subUrbia,* for example, who knows what he doesn't want to do but hasn't quite put together yet what he wants to do. Can you talk a little bit about that idea, because I know you've come back to that in a couple of different characters?

RL: I keep coming back to it, just because it's such a poignant time in someone's life, and I was amazed at the things you're up against. It was clear to me at the time—when you're a teenager and you're like that, it's kind of charming and people understand, but once you're college age and beyond, society and your parents and everybody have zero sympathy. The culture has such contempt for some young person who doesn't have it all together, or have a bunch of ambition—sanctioned ambition, you know, that they approve of. I always had a soft spot for young people who are trying to figure it out and looking for something—they want a more interesting life than going to business school or whatever would make their parents happy. Jeff is the embodiment of that, but to varying degrees, Sooze certainly is too. She's artistic and wants to express herself; she's got all that ambition. But you know, that's not bad, too, at that age—it's a lot of ego, and that's an offshoot of it. So, yeah, it was about that. Very dramatic too—the piece had a lot more drama than would be my inclination. By the end, there's guns out; the heat rises in it, which I like. It starts out pretty banal, and just builds, builds, builds. I love the trajectory of that. And I think that's when I realized as a writer I probably need goosing in that direction—that's not how I usually think. *Before Sunrise* arguably builds, but towards a first kiss, in very antidramatic ways, where [on *subUrbia*] it was fun to have that structure. And it was the first time I had done something that didn't really originate with me. I thought, if I'm going to do this a long time . . . I'm going to do things that are outside myself that I find my way into; that's only natural. But that was the first time I had.

DJ: With *The Newton Boys,* what drew you to that project initially?

RL: It's one of those things—it's like, what draws you to anything in this world? What draws you to a story? I just saw myself in those characters. I loved that it was a true story; I loved the time period, the way it segued from Old West to modern times. By the late teens and twenties, the culture was very modern, but if you lived in West Texas, it wasn't—it might as well have been 1870, practically. Those guys, the trajectory of their own lives was pretty breathtaking, to go from dirt to big-city Chicago, so I loved the arc of that. . . .

If people said, "What's the one film of yours that you think is underrated?" I would say *Newton Boys,* because by the time it came out, there were various reasons it felt like it was stacked against us. Matthew [McConaughey] was suffering backlash; he had become a big star in the meantime, and some people felt, unfairly, [an] overnight success— "Okay, we're going to bring him down," so we were caught in that tide. There was some perception of, why are you doing this movie? This isn't the kind of movie you do. It was like I had sold out, even though I was one of the writers on the movie, I optioned it with my own money, [and] it's a very close-to-home story—Texas. They wouldn't have said that to an Italian filmmaker, making a film about some gangster from 1920—"Oh, this is his culture"—but if you're from Texas, no one put that together. . . .

Newton Boys actually tested really well—it tested better than *Dazed* and better than other films I had done. . . . We had four previews, and twenty people stay after each preview. And the first thing they ask is, "Well, how many of you like the movie, a show of hands?" Four screenings—eighty hands went up. Not one person said they didn't like the movie. And I remember talking to Peter Rice at Fox; I'm like, "Isn't it good, everybody likes it?" He goes, "Yeah, people like it, but here's the problem: they don't *love* it." And I go, well . . . it ends with them going off to prison; I don't know if they're supposed to love it, but it's a fun journey; I want to hang out with these guys for two hours. And they're like, "Eh, that's not good enough, you know. People aren't going to recommend it as much; you need a movie that people *love.* It's not enough love." I said, I'll take all of those likes . . . you know who likes that movie? People I know—construction workers, southern people. It was for the CMT crowd. It's not for New York and L.A.; it's really for the flyover, middle America. It's these country boys beating the big-city boys at their own game. That got totally lost, totally lost. . . .

It did not satisfy people's bloodlust, too. These guys didn't want to kill people; they weren't psychopaths, you know? I mean, Willis Newton thought Bonnie and Clyde were morons. I actually met Arthur Penn once in New York, and we were talking, and he had heard of *Newton Boys,* because it just had been out a couple months, and he asked me about it. I said, yeah, it's kind of my anti–*Bonnie and Clyde,* because Willis Newton, the main character, says, Bonnie and Clyde, they were these silly kids, if someone got in front of them, they shot at them—bound to get themselves killed. And Arthur Penn looked at me and goes, "He's right!"—he just had a smile on his face—"He's right, they were crazy." That's who goes down in history: the body-count guys. But I find it much more heroic to have pretty much gotten away with it, and to not have hurt anybody. To me that fits into a proper ethic. They really did what they set out to do successfully, and they brought all of their technology and intellect and cunning and *cojones* to that, and they achieved it, you know? My kind of criminals. The kind of criminal I would be, or have been.

DJ: To go to *Waking Life,* how did you prepare for writing that film?

RL: Well, *Waking Life* was very similar in some cyclical, life-spiraling-back-to-itself kind of way to *Slacker.* I mean, I was coming from a similar place; I was unable to get other films made. I'd gone down the road a couple times post–*Newton Boys,* films I just couldn't get financing for . . . *Rivethead, Friday Night Lights,* and some other things. No one would pull the trigger on anything. . . .

So I saw Tommy [Pallotta] and Bob [Sabiston's] shorts they were working on; they had been developing that animation technique over the years—Bob's software. I had seen that when it was black-and-white. Little drawings—they had done some interstitials for MTV. And then they had jumped to color, and it had gotten a little more sophisticated. And they were just showing me like their latest stuff, and something clicked in my mind: this film I had been thinking about, literally for twenty years, taking notes on, and it had never worked. . . . Someone said, the most important films you make are the ones you make in your head, but never make, because if you can finish it, it's done; it's not that interesting. *Waking Life* was just . . . a movie in search of a form, for all these years. Even before I was a filmmaker, it was just a story I was working on, more or less real events. It became my decade, kitchen-sink movie that I could put everything into, in some way or another. I really just pored through notebooks and started fashioning up this story. It was fun to get excited about that. I felt like I was back to zero, going from a twenty-seven-million-dollar studio film, Cinemascope, to shooting with a little digital camera and a sound guy. . . .

It felt like maybe my last movie; it was either going to be my last movie or my first new movie. There was a lot of newness. Maybe it was the millennial thing. There was just something, a certain energy that I felt with that movie that it was very special and couldn't be more personal. It was pretty awesome to bring those same methods into such a crazy movie. . . . I didn't have a technical script; I had like forty-five, fifty pages of notes with outlines and ideas. And I could sit down and articulate as best I could, but I talked about it really as a process. . . . Ultimately, it's a film that's becoming aware of itself as a film on some level. That all felt formally and spiritually aligned there, so it was . . . a good creative reassessing moment that I think I needed at that very moment.

DJ: Well, it does seem to tie in organically with *Tape,* with your using the digital cameras in that environment, even though you are working off a play. . . .

RL: Yeah, I had finished *Waking Life,* and we were in that yearlong animation process. I don't think I would have undertaken it had I not shot *Waking Life* digitally . . . even though for *Waking Life,* it was sort of a capture medium. It didn't really matter; it just was convenient. But as I did that—because, you know, you edit it, live-action—I said, if I ever made a movie, here's how I could do it. And I'm always quick to say, not every movie should look like this, but if it's the right subject matter, it fits.

And then Ethan sent me this play that he had done a reading to, but at this point, no one had seen it. He sent it to me, and we got to talking about it as a film. I got excited about it, and it happened fairly quickly. And it's funny—I was shooting those more than a year apart, even though they came out around the same time. They were both in the same theater. I remember it was the Lincoln Plaza—there were certain theaters that they were both playing at the same time. My little Clifford Odets moment . . . but I put them in different years altogether, because *Waking Life* had not only had a twenty-year gestation but had so much prep work, and then the shooting of it—it was so sprawling and outgoing. And then *Tape* is, boom: one room, three people, go! They're very different, but it was pushing that digital storytelling, trying to work within that or expand on what I felt I learned on *Waking Life.* It was great. And the sheer dramatic challenge of that is something I felt I had been working up to forever. You know, I always joked—people were like, "Oh, your movies take place in like twenty-four hours or eighteen hours or twelve." They don't all, but yeah, I get what you're saying. Well, I always joked that, someday, I'll make a real-time movie, so this is that. You know, how to really deal with a real-time situation—I had no idea. I thought that would be the only one, and two years later I'm shooting *Before Sunset*—that exactly again, a real-time movie. I wouldn't have thought I'd ever have two real-time movies. It was a joke at various points in the '90s when I'd be asked about that, but it became a reality.

DJ: Some of your films have talked really directly about time. The beginning of *Before Sunset* where Jesse is talking about that book he's going to write that all takes place in the space of a pop song, or *Waking Life,* your character at the end talks about that.

RL: Yeah, it is an interesting notion—time as a subject, it's fascinating on all its levels. And then, time in relation to cinema is particularly fascinating, if you think of it as maybe the most unique element of film as an art form is the time, how you structure the time. The way you can manipulate time—slow down, speed it up, jump it around—there's a time element that doesn't quite exist in other art forms in the same way. In a book, the author can have your story span whatever time you want, but the reader can control that by how quick or slow they read it. Now, in a film that's meant to be seen assumingly in one pass, what you do with the time and the viewer's time is interesting. You know, music unfolds in time. And, so, it's always intrigued me, and time and narrative have always been overlapping constants that are worthy of exploration.

DJ: Going back now, I actually thought of one of your films when the "Ground Zero mosque" stuff started happening: *Life from Shiva's Dance*

Floor. . . . [When you made it], there were already some other proposals on the table, if they hadn't already been voted on, isn't that right?

RL: There were still a bunch of proposals; nothing had been firmed up. It was a big mess. For all I know it still is one, or maybe they've come up with something. So, yeah, that was in the air. There was talk about other filmmakers—there were all these kind of omnibus films where different filmmakers were responding. It was such a big event—you get invited to do these things. And so, Speed is a dear friend, and we had both gone down to the Ground Zero just the week or two after, together, and walked around . . . we were at the New York Film Festival for *Waking Life,* and we walked around and talked a little about that. And then just over the next month, we talked about that.

DJ: And had you done one of his cruises before?

RL: You know, I hadn't, not officially, but as a friend just walking around New York with him, [it] becomes that, you know. I kind of had and hadn't. And he had a very specific Wall Street, World Trade-Center tour, so it was parts of that, tying it into 9/11 and the World Trade Center, so it worked out really nice. The thing was, it was fundamentally scripted. It was sort of a documentary, but it was rehearsed and the sections were all laid out. It wasn't by any means a traditional documentary where you just start shooting and see what happens.

Speed's take on things resonates with me. . . . He's a great performer, thinker, writer—all of the above.

DJ: Well, he actually shows up in your next film, *School of Rock.* (I'm going in order of release here . . .) *School of Rock* was definitely a critically successful film, but financially successful too. And I'm just curious, when you experience some measure of . . .

RL: That rarity of rarities, where you can get both critical acceptance and, you know, box office. [*Laughs.*]

DJ: [*Laughs.*] Does the box-office success give you some extended freedom and open doors, or not?

RL: You know, it's never put to you on such terms—well, if you do this, then you can do that. (They're never the same people offering you, so it's not like, oh, I made them that, you know . . .)

At this point in life, I had a lot of turning points and a lot of new steps—when I came out of both *Waking Life* and *Tape,* I felt new in some way, like I was ready for different challenges. I wasn't so closed off and paranoid about how things could go wrong; I was thinking more positive—like how things could go right. I turned down all these films over the years just because I felt, oh, it will get screwed up . . . so I don't want to do it. It sounds like a bad experience. But I was thinking positive, and *School of Rock* came my way. And [Scott] Rudin really felt I was the guy to do it; he was pretty obsessed. He knew I could do something with it and make it what it wanted to be . . . so, with Jack [Black]—who was already attached, of course—Mike [White] and myself, the three of us got together in our own ways and made that the film it wanted to be. I felt I had a great creative experience on that. It was just the opposite of what you think when you hear "studio film": a bunch of guys telling you what to do, not listening to you. I found the power of the director, really. I had been afraid of that before—like, you do a studio film, you lose your power. And this was, no, you get to exert your power. . . . I brought the indie spirit of everything I had done and was able to pull it off at a studio level. It was fun. . . .

You know, for me, *School of Rock*'s about that character, Dewey. Jack's character, there are elements of him that are very close to me . . . and then the music, of course, a guy who's passionate about something. I felt he was kind of a slacker from my earlier films. He's a little older now but has his passion, and it's like, where does that passion fit into the world? Well, it kind of doesn't, and it kind of does, if used correctly. So when people accused a lot of my characters from years before of being lazy or not very productive, I was like, well, actually, I don't know if I agree with that. I think they can be. It's just finding the right outlet. That's what people really do in this world. You find what you're good at and passionate about. You know, if you're lucky, there's a job in there. You can do it. So, by the end of the movie, when he's teaching that class, that's kind of wonderful.

DJ: And the film that follows this is *Before Sunset*. We've talked about collaboration and all the writing that you all did on [*Before Sunrise*] together. When you really started getting serious about making that again, and you really started to trade ideas, is there any moment in the finished film that you could point to as an example and say here's what I contributed, here's what Julie contributed, what Ethan contributed, or is it so organic a process that by the end it's just everyone's contribution together?

RL: There's a lot of overlap there. As a team, three is a good number because if two of us really like something and the third doesn't like it, usually, it's not in the movie at all. It just doesn't fit if all three of us aren't on board with the thoughts, sentiments, and whatever it is that's in the air. It's a good sounding board. I mean, I had things that I felt so strongly about or I felt were where I was at, at the time, trying to articulate it. If Julie or Ethan . . . didn't get what I was trying to express, then it just falls out of the movie. And likewise. I think once we really discovered what this film was—the idea of it, and the three of us, agreed on that—then it was really just a matter of six months to a year just emailing each other and writing, back and forth. They'd send me long things; I'd edit it and I'd throw out ideas; it was just kind of everybody, it was this hodgepodge. As director, I was often in the role of writer and an editor of their stuff. But it was interesting.

We were all a little afraid. Diving into that was very intimidating—characters we cared about, something we felt was certainly special to all of us, having done it, those years before in Vienna. The pressure of doing a sequel—like I said, no one wanted a second film. There wasn't anyone clamoring for it; no one wanted to do it. We had kind of the same budget we had in Vienna nine years earlier. So we just had to jump in, and we shot that in fifteen days. Shot *Tape* in six. This is an era in the films where I was like, okay, you just have to make films. This is when my admiration for Fassbinder really kicked in; you say, how did Fassbinder make all those films? Well, he shot that in fourteen days, and then he edited it, and it was like, okay, it can be done. You just really have to have it going in; you really have to have a plan. And that has served me well—actually, in the film I just wrapped. Twenty-two days: go. You do it. So, *Sunset,* that's kind of what we had—[we] made it work. I ran from the mix—I'd just finished the mix of *School of Rock* in New York at Sound One, got on a plane, went to Paris, had about five weeks of preproduction, and then shot that in fifteen days and then came back before *School of Rock* came out, in time for the junket. So, it was really cool. When *School of Rock* opened, I was already in postproduction on *Before Sunset.*

DJ: Is that an ideal way of working for you?

RL: Yeah, yeah. It's really great. I felt blessed, really, to just be able to go from one project to the next.

DJ: And you had already shot *Scanner* before you shot *Bad News Bears,* is that correct?

RL: Yeah, after I was back from Paris in postproduction on *Before Sunset,* I shot an HBO pilot that I had written called *$5.15/Hr.* That was fun. But they chose not to pick it up, so, I was like, okay, I'll put all that . . . into *Fast Food Nation* someday. In the meantime, when they didn't pick it up, I was happy because I thought I could get *Scanner Darkly* finally made. I had been trying to get that off the ground for a while. It looked like the planets might be lining up on that. So I was happy to go right into that in the spring of '04 . . . that was the order: it was *Sunset, $5.15, Scanner.* And then I had shot *Scanner* and edited it, and the animation had begun—much more detailed than *Waking Life,* a different animation methodology. And it was going to take a lot longer to do, and that's where it gets a little slow for me . . . so when they sent *Bad News Bears* to me, I thought it was so funny—bold that they were trying to do a remake of this crazy film. I just started getting interested in that. But it worked out well in my life too to go do that while the animation was going on. It ended up coming out before *Scanner,* but in my mind, it was after. The things I had done were pretty adult, pretty serious, especially *Scanner*—I mean, that's some darker material. It was fun to jump into a baseball comedy, as far as what I needed next.

I loved Buttermaker obviously—Billy's character felt in some parallel universe close to me [*laughs*] . . . and the baseball-ness of it. What the music was in *School of Rock,* the baseball was in *Bears* to me personally. As a former player, I was like, okay, I really know the baseball—I really wanted to bring that. And so we shot that next; I was editing that as *Scanner* was still being worked on. I went straight from that to *Fast Food Nation.* And then it was *Fast Food Nation* and *Scanner* that came to the finish line at the same time. So, there's a lot crammed in there. But it tells you how long *Scanner* took, that I shot two other movies from the time I shot *Scanner,* and one of them came out around the same time.

DJ: Speaking of the dark subject matter of *Scanner,* I know you've talked about how the politics of it reflect that moment in 2006 as much as it does Dick's of the early to midseventies. Thinking about the novel and Dick's dystopian visions—I know this is always a strange guess to venture with any writer—what do you think he would have to say about either what was happening in 2006 or what's happening in 2010?

RL: Well, I think it would have just proven to him how right he was. I've said a few times along the way, paranoia and conspiracy theory plus a generation equals often the reality. You know, global warming was a joke. In the early '80s I remember hearing it—late '70s, early '80s—it was, like, oh, the polar ice caps melt; they're going to flood. It was just like one of those things you almost joke about. And in *Slacker,* it was used as a paranoid joke. Even though everyone grasped the underlying reality of it, the people who were shouting the loudest about it seemed like cranks and kooks, right? That's how they come off. And then it gets more sanctioned and accredited as time and science catch up. It's just funny the way the paranoid person has a receptor out that hears something, maybe hears something about a study or [that] has a basis in science, and Philip K. Dick was obviously all over the science of everything. It would lead into more of an imaginative world, and he would jump to some much-farther-down-the-road conclusion. The way he would grab a piece of fact and then run with it—that's how the schizophrenic or a paranoid person who is not an artist does it too, you know, the people you run into who are just on fire about some issue. There usually is a percent that is grounded in something real, so I've always been interested in the paranoid, the conspiracy theory, all that. . . .

We're living in science fiction right now: cell phones, communication, it's just exponentially growing. I think the reality of our moment, the surveillance state, the post-9/11 paranoia, all that infused updating *Scanner.* The war on terror becomes this war on drugs, where they overlap. And the narco-state, the paranoia, the surveillance, all that, was so sanctioned, at that point—it was official policy in the government at some point in there. So, Philip K. Dick would be, to answer your question, he'd be light-years ahead, taking these things to deeper, darker conclusions. But he'd be twenty years ahead, at least.

DJ: I'm thinking about something that you and Eric Schlosser talk about in relation to *Fast Food Nation,* when you talk about that idea of these structures, whether it's a government structure or a corporate structure, as a kind of a machine unto itself, so that you have this situation where you think that these are really good people—like Don in *Fast Food Nation,* you know, is basically a good guy.

RL: Yeah, he's not a bad guy.

DJ: And yet the decisions he's making, the decisions that a lot of these people are making, are inflicting harm on these workers at the slaughterhouses and inflicting harm on the consumer. Do you see this is a conundrum that we can work our way out of as a culture—that's a big question, I know—or is this just the state of things?

RL: I think my bigger thinking and Eric's was that humans, we're just a small part of these bigger machines. What is individuality? What does it even mean, you know? This is a deep question we all have to live with every day of our lives. And does what you purchase at the store matter? Do your choices matter? Where do you take a stand? And, yeah, Don, he's a totally decent guy. And that's the banality of evil. You know, some guy going to work at Auschwitz and going home to get his paycheck and feed his family. Who's to say he wasn't a decent guy? Some low-level bureaucrat or guard at Auschwitz—like, could it be? Of course it could be. Not only could it be, but it was. No one goes through the world with a pitchfork saying, "I'm evil incarnate." Hitler himself was a charming guy who could be persuasive and tell people what they want to hear. The truly evil people in the world, the psychopaths, they're in prison or they take themselves out. The worst is the sociopath who soars to the top of his field. Whether it's politics, someone like Dick Cheney . . . they really don't have empathy and they don't care, but they're smart. They can do well on Wall Street, these people who do the most damage. They end up leaders and CEOs because they are sure of themselves and they don't apologize. That's who you want leading the charge for the shareholders. But they're still charming and intelligent and can sit down and have a meeting. And that's the dangerous sociopath . . . the CEO may or may not be one, but the corporation itself, by definition, almost is. It doesn't have feelings for anybody; it's there strictly for its own needs and would only care about any other needs only insofar as it has to legally. The only deterrent is that it could get busted and cost the shareholders. But that's as far it goes; they're just a voracious machine. So it was just interesting to see people caught up in the various elements in this, the systems that are bigger than all of us and always will be.

You know, even the presidency is bigger than the individual, as Obama has learned. [*Laughs.*] I mean, actually Obama knew it going in. Give him credit. He knew it. All the delusional people around him, all of us, who every cycle delude ourselves that one person's going to make a huge difference—you know, you can't; the system is there. So it's, can you reform the system? Can you do it? And what's it worth to you? I don't know—it was fascinating stuff. Greg Kinnear, we talked a lot about that part. Don is not a bad guy, and he compromises and . . . I don't know. It was funny that—and we got shit for it—but when he chooses not to have a backbone or stand up, or the way he just walks out of the movie. That was a narrative conceit which I thought was really pretty radical, if you think about it: that the guy who's the lead character walks through those doors and leaves everyone else just floating in this world. That's when you realize that the machine is bigger than any individual. I had to win that one over people, because they said, "Can he come back?" And I said, "Well, we had an idea for him at the very end," but the point was that he went out of the narrative. I said, "It's like *Psycho*—Janet Leigh, she's the star, and then she's gone. You pick up with everybody else." So, I did that. But I remember there were a couple reviews, they saw it as a flaw—messy, you know. They didn't get that element that we were trying to say with that. He's just one of the stories, a touching one for a guy who has worked his way up and could potentially make a difference, but there's always going to be a guy like the Bruce Willis character, who is much more practical and vaguely threatening, not to mention cynical.

You can take any issue, and I, like most people, fluctuate between cynicism and disparity over things and this kind of optimism that things can change, so I don't know. You can feel it being worked out in the movie. And some people think the movie is a real bummer, and then others felt like it changed them in some way, that they would never look at that the same. I think that's optimistic whenever you see a bigger picture of a system. That can only be positive. That's why I'm basically optimistic. This era—the information that's out there. I like WikiLeaks. I like all that. The more the information, the more you can, as Bill Hicks would say, squeegee your eyes and see what's going on. To put it together and maybe make sense of it a little bit; the more people who can understand things, the more things shift. It's always been power's key element to maintain this power is people just not caring or not understanding at all. A not very curious population is the ideal. It's the least threatening.

DJ: Let me switch gears for a second and—this is going to take us to a completely different mind-set—ask you about *Inning by Inning*.

RL: . . . I'm a fan of documentaries that are portraits. *The Cruise* is a portrait of Speed, but it's actually more of a portrait of Bennett Miller than it is Speed, ultimately, if you know them. You realize once you get to know Speed that, oh, it's really more about Bennett. That was Bennett's take on Speed, which is about 180 degrees off from where Speed is, although fascinating, fascinating. But that brings up the question, can you really capture anyone? You know, I've seldom liked it when I've seen myself, an article about me or some attempt at a profile—it's just, scraping the surface and getting that wrong, too. It's pretty much an impossible task. And that's the line from *Scanner,* dying knowing little and getting that part wrong too: that's my vision of communication or summing up anything to do with a person. You *will* be wrong. So, given that, I approached Augie with this idea: trying to follow the team for a season and see where that took us. They had just won the national championship the year before, and he had said he had never repeated. It's very hard to repeat. And of course, they had a lot of guys coming back. They were ranked number one. I thought, well, if they win it again or go to Omaha, that will be interesting; if they don't, that will be interesting. I just felt like that was a good year to follow them. And sure enough, it was kind of an underachieving year where they lost in the playoffs and did not make it back to the World Series, but I had so much footage of him that I segued and just made a portrait of him, through some interviews, talks with other people. It became this portrait of him that wasn't geared to any one season or anything . . . and I warned him in advance this is going to be a portrait of me to a degree—I got that on the table. It will be things that I find interesting, that I can relate to. At one point I let him know, that one time you yelled at the team, I want to leave that in there even though I know it's tough—I gave it a lot of context—because I think I have to do that in what I do, every now and then. Maybe once a movie. Maybe one every two, three movies. I've got to let it really be known that the leader here—me—cares. And if you're not with it, there's the door. . . .

DJ: Well, let me then ask you about *Me and Orson Welles,* which seems like a real fit with your interests.

RL: Oh, yeah, it really clicked. Again, what draws you to material that you're not originating? And it's like, well, so much here. I always told people I felt I might not ever have a film about making a film, but making a film about putting on a play was very similar to the part I would like to deal with. And that's those inner dynamics, the creative process, creating art in a group setting—it's personal, you know. That's what theater and film are—they're collaborative, open, process mediums, no matter what anybody says. A whole lot of parts, a lot of moving parts, a lot of personalities—all that stuff is fascinating. And then, how interesting to meet Welles at a point in his life that few people know much about? You know, there's no real records. I mean, there's pictures, but there's not moving images much from that era in his life. And it's kind of glossed over in the Welles bio: young prodigy, *War of the Worlds, Citizen Kane.* They jump over this incredible period he had in New York theater—vibrant, earth-shattering. What he did really changed things, and it was huge.

A lot of movies, when they do theater, it's always a bad production of something. A lot of my theater friends [said], "Oh, finally, a film that doesn't make us all look like idiots." You know, it's so much easier to do films about bad theater. Everyone can laugh and get together and say, oh, that sucks. And even the actors would ask me, "Well, am I good actor?" And I was like, oh, yeah, you're good . . . I was like, here's our bar: this is the best Shakespeare production in North American history, the most historical, and people are still talking about it seventy-one years later, so, the actor in it, if Welles and John Houseman cast you, you were the best person, and they are probably better than you are, so let's take it from there. There was no safety net; the bar was pretty high. It was a lot of fun to try to re-create that moment, to historically bring that back to life. The key to that, of course, is getting Christian McKay, finding him—that's the key to that movie working or not, obviously. You're not going to misrepresent Welles or do anything less than, and I wouldn't have done it had the film gods not offered him up.

But it was a wonderful experience. I think that the indie film world or international was ending. It's like the last one through the closing window. Even from the time we started that to the time we finished it, the world had changed in the indie world. All of these companies out of business, no more financing. I felt like it was like the last one of its kind.

DJ: Has that affected the direction you want to go from here—thinking about that window closing?

RL: It closed, so some things I was hoping to do right after that, I haven't been able to. I had a college comedy I'm trying to do, and you suddenly can't get funding for anything else. I was very happy to get this recent film made with Jack Black, a comedy. There's so little money . . . I don't know, it's a shifting world out there. But filmmakers always adapt and make things work for them. And humans are so adaptable to begin with, so artists within that have to find a way. It's interesting, you know. I look back and I go—when people are complaining about it, and everybody is, I mean, everybody—for people anywhere in my generation, I look at them and go, "Yeah, things suck now, but we had a pretty good run there. I got a lot of films made that just wouldn't have a chance in hell in getting made today, so that feels [like] pretty good timing, and I don't feel sorry for you." [But] if you're in your twenties now, and just starting out, not only are there no companies interested in financing or helping you, there's not even an audience out there for these kinds of smaller stories.

DJ: I read about a project you're doing about a boy growing up, and it's shooting once a year, is that correct?

RL: Yeah, yeah. That's a work in progress.

DJ: Is that still ongoing?

RL: Yeah, I'm about to shoot year nine.

DJ: How many years total do you want to do?

RL: Twelve years; I'm following a kid through his public education. But it's fiction. It's not a documentary or anything like that. I was just trying to make a film about childhood, and I couldn't quite figure out what point of childhood. Like *400 Blows,* pick a few days in the life of a kid: what age? I had so much I felt to express about that whole process, so I got that once, every now and then, what feels like a completely original idea of, *what if I . . . ?* You know, I'm always thinking about how to tell a story. You have your subject matter, but then, what's the right form for it is the issue. So I had this idea to just film a little bit every year. Talk about time in cinema . . . It's a year later, and everyone is getting older. In the young people, you see it pretty dramatically, the boy and his sister. The parents, played by Patricia Arquette and Ethan Hawke—they're divorced parents—a little less, but they change a lot too. So it's been a really fun process. I think time is sort of a lead character, if you wanted to get technical about it—the lead character of the movie.

DJ: Tell me a little bit about *Bernie* and what you have been most pleased with on this project.

RL: Oh, well, I'm really excited about it. It was a *Texas Monthly* article I read when I was working on *Newton Boys* in '97—I was in post on that and finishing that film in '98. It's a very strange true-crime story—funny, though. And very much set in East Texas where I grew up, in Huntsville. . . . [It's been] ten years in the works—I went to the trial back in '99. And it's been one of those things I've been feeling my way through. Finally, it all happened—again, a very low budget, everyone working for scale—the typical thing to get anything personal made these days. So, again, I'm happy to have gotten that made, but it just gets tougher and tougher, so I don't know. I think it's one at a time now. Each time I'm kind of amazed it gets in, you know, like, alright—I get to make another!

Principal and some supporting cast listed, with the exceptions of *It's Impossible, Slacker,* and *Waking Life,* where all cast has been credited. Experimental films made prior to 1989 are not included, nor are the currently unavailable video *Heads I Win/Tails You Lose* (1991) and the unreleased HBO pilot *$5.15/Hr.* (2004). Films dated according to year of U.S. domestic theatrical release, with the exceptions of *Live from Shiva's Dance Floor,* released on DVD, and *Inning by Inning,* released on the ESPN cable-television network.

It's Impossible to Learn to Plow by Reading Books (1989)
USA
Production: Detour Filmproduction
Direction: Richard Linklater
Conception: Richard Linklater
Cinematography: Richard Linklater
Editing: Richard Linklater
Cast: Richard Linklater, James Goodwin, Daniel Kratochvil, Linda Finney, Tracy Crabtree, Linda Levine, Lisa Schiebold, Erin MacAfee, Various Family, D. Montgomery, Scott Van Horn, Daniel Johnston, Tammy Gomez, Keith McCormack
Color
86 min.

Slacker (1991)
USA
Production: Detour Filmproduction
Producer: Richard Linklater
Distribution: Orion Classics
Direction: Richard Linklater
Screenplay: Richard Linklater

Cinematography: Lee Daniel

Editing: Scott Rhodes

Casting: Anne Walker-McBay

Cast: Richard Linklater (Should have stayed at bus station), Rudy Basquez (Taxi Driver), Jean Caffeine (Roadkill), Jan Hockey (Jogger), Stephan Hockey (Running late), Mark James (Hit-and-run son), Samuel Dietert (Grocery grabber of death's bounty), Bob Boyd (Officer Bozzio), Terrence Kirk (Officer Love), Keith McCormack (Street musician), Jennifer Schaudies (Walking to coffee shop), Dan Kratochvil (Espresso czar), Maris Strautmanis (Giant cappuccino), Brecht Andersch (Dostoyevsky wannabe), Tom Pallotta (Looking for missing friend), Jerry Deloney (Been on the moon since the 50's), Heather West (Tura Satana look-alike), John Spath (Co-op guy), Ron Marks (Bush basher), Daniel Dugan (Comb game player), Brian Crockett (Sadistic comb game player), Scott Marcus (Ultimate loser), Stella Weir (Stephanie from Dallas), Teresa Taylor (Pap smear pusher), Mark Harris (T-shirt terrorist), Greg Wilson (Anti-traveller), Debbie Pastor (Wants to leave country), Gina Lalli (Sidewalk psychic), Sharon Roos (Devoted follower), Frank Orrall (Happy-go-lucky guy), Skip Fulton Jr. (Two for one special), Abra Moore (Has change), Lori Capp (Traumatized yacht owner), Gus Vayas (Cranky cook), Louis Black (Paranoid paper reader), Don Stroud (Recluse in bathrobe), Janelle Coolich (Shut-in girlfriend), Aleister Barron (Peeping kid), Albans Benchoff (Coke machine robber), Nigel Benchoff (Budding capitalist youth), Zara Barron (Coke heist accomplice), Kevin Whitley (Jilted boyfriend), Steve Anderson (Guy who tosses typewriter), Robert Pierson (Based on authoritative sources), Sarah Harmon (Has faith in groups), David Haymond (Street dweller), John Slate ("Conspiracy A-Go-Go" author), Scott Van Horn (Nova), Lee Daniel (GTO), Charles Gunning (Hitchhiker awaiting "true call"), Tamsy Ringler (Video interviewer), Luke Savisky (Video cameraman), Meg Brennan (Sitting at cafe), Phillip Hostak (Hit up for cigarettes), D. Angus MacDonald (Video playing store security), Shelly Kristaponis (Shoplifter), Louis Mackey (Old anarchist), Kathy McCarty (Anarchist's daughter), Michael Laird (Burglar), Jack Meredith (Get-away accomplice), Clark Lee Walker (Cadillac crook), Kalman Spellitich (Video backpacker), Siqgouri Wilkovich (Slapping boyfriend), John Hawkins (Choking girlfriend), Scott Rhodes (Disgruntled grad student), Denise Montgomery (Having a breakthrough day), Mimi Vitetta (Teacup sculptor), Susannah Simone (Working on same painting), Bruce Hughes (Card playing waiter), Keith Fletcher (Cafe card player #1), Eric Buehlman (Cafe card player #2), R. Malice (Scooby Doo philosopher), Mark Quirk (Papa Smurf), Kim Krizan (Questions happiness), Annick Souhami (Has conquered fear of rejection), Regina

Garza (Smoking writer), Stephen Jacobson (S-T-E-V-E with a van), Eric Lord (Doorman at club), Kelly Linn (Bike rider with nice shoes), Rachael Reinhardt (Cousin from Greece), Stewart Bennet (Sitting on ledge), Kevin Thompson (Handstamping arm licker), Nick Maffei (Pixl-Visionary), Nolan Morrison (To be buried by history), Dan Kratochvil (Masonic malcontent), Kyle Rosenblad (Going to catch a show), Ed Hall (Band playing at club), Lucinda Scott (Dairy Queen photographer), Wammo (Anti-artist), Marianne Hyatt (Late night pick-up), Gary Price (Watching early morning TV), Joseph Jones (Old man recording thoughts), Kendal Smith (Postmodern Paul Revere), Sean Coffey (Super 8 cameraman), Jennifer Carroll (All-night partier), Charlotte Norris (Convertible driver), Patrice Sullivan (Day tripper), Greg Ward (Tosses camera off cliff)
Color
100 min.

Dazed and Confused (1993)
USA
Production: Alphaville, Detour Filmproduction
Producers: James Jacks, Sean Daniel, Richard Linklater, and Anne Walker-McBay
Distribution: Universal/Gramercy Pictures
Direction: Richard Linklater
Screenplay: Richard Linklater
Cinematography: Lee Daniel
Editing: Sandra Adair
Production Design: John Frick
Costume Design: Katherine (K. D.) Dover
Casting: Don Phillips
Cast: Jason London (Pink), Joey Lauren Adams (Simone), Milla Jovovich (Michelle), Shawn Andrews (Pickford), Rory Cochrane (Slater), Adam Goldberg (Mike), Anthony Rapp (Tony), Sasha Jenson (Don), Marissa Ribisi (Cynthia), Deena Martin (Shavonne), Michelle Burke (Jodi), Cole Hauser (Benny), Christine Harnos (Kaye), Wiley Wiggins (Mitch), Mark Vandermeulen (Tommy), Esteban Powell (Carl), Jeremy Fox (Hirshfelder), Ben Affleck (O'Bannion), Jason O. Smith (Melvin), Christin Hinojosa (Sabrina), Parker Posey (Darla), Matthew McConaughey (Wooderson), Catherine Morris (Julie), Nicky Katt (Clint), Rick Moser (Assistant Coach), Terry G. Mross (Coach Conrad)
Color
102 min.

Before Sunrise (1995)
Austria and USA
Production: Castle Rock Entertainment, Detour Filmproduction,
    F.I.L.M.H.A.U.S., Wien
Producers: Ellen Winn Wendl, Gernot Schaffler, Wolfgang Ramml, John
    Sloss, Anne Walker-McBay, Gregory Jacobs
Distribution: Columbia Pictures
Direction: Richard Linklater
Screenplay: Richard Linklater, Kim Krizan
Cinematography: Lee Daniel
Editing: Sandra Adair
Production Design: Florian Reichmann
Costume Design: Florentina Welley
Casting: Judy Henderson, Alycia Aumuller
Cast: Ethan Hawke (Jesse), Julie Delpy (Celine), Andrea Eckert (Wife on
    Train), Hanno Pöschl (Husband on Train), Karl Bruckschwaiger and Tex
    Rubinowitz (Guys on Bridge), Erni Mangold (Palm Reader), Dominik
    Castell (Street Poet), Haymon Maria Buttinger (Bartender)
Color
101 min.

subUrbia (1997)
USA
Production: Castle Rock Entertainment, Detour Filmproduction
Producers: John Sloss, Anne Walker-McBay
Distribution: Sony Pictures Classics
Direction: Richard Linklater
Screenplay: Eric Bogosian
Cinematography: Lee Daniel
Editing: Sandra Adair
Production Design: Catherine Hardwicke
Costume Design: Melanie Armstrong
Music Supervisor: Randall Poster
Casting: Judy Henderson, Alycia Aumuller
Cast: Jayce Bartok (Pony), Amie Carey (Sooze), Nicky Katt (Tim), Ajay
    Naidu (Nazeer), Parker Posey (Erica), Giovanni Ribisi (Jeff), Samia Shoaib
    (Pakeesa), Dina Spybey (Bee-Bee), Steve Zahn (Buff)
Color
121 min.

The Newton Boys (1998)
USA
Production: Twentieth Century–Fox, Detour Filmproduction
Producers: John Sloss, Anne Walker-McBay, Clark Lee Walker, Keith
　Fletcher
Distribution: Twentieth Century–Fox
Direction: Richard Linklater
Screenplay: Richard Linklater, Claude Stanush, Clark Lee Walker
Cinematography: Peter James
Editing: Sandra Adair
Production Design: Catherine Hardwicke
Costume Design: Shelley Komarov
Casting: Don Phillips
Cast: Matthew McConaughey (Willis Newton), Ethan Hawke (Jess Newton),
　Skeet Ulrich (Joe Newton), Vincent D'Onofrio (Dock Newton), Dwight
　Yoakam (Brentwood Glasscock), Julianna Margulies (Louise Brown), Bo
　Hopkins (K. P. Aldrich), Chloe Webb (Avis Glasscock), Charles Gunning
　(Slim), Luke Askew (Chief Schoemaker)
Color
122 min.

Waking Life (2001)
USA
Production: Fox Searchlight Pictures, the Independent Film Channel,
　Thousand Words, Flat Black Films, Detour Filmproduction
Producers: Anne Walker-McBay, Tommy Pallotta, Palmer West, Jonah Smith,
　Jonathan Sehring, Caroline Kaplan, John Sloss
Distribution: Fox Searchlight Pictures
Direction: Richard Linklater
Screenplay: Richard Linklater
Cinematography: Richard Linklater, Tommy Pallotta
Editing: Sandra Adair
Art Direction: Bob Sabiston
Music: Tosca Tango Orchestra
Original Score: Glover Gill
Sound Supervision/Sound Design: Tom Hammond
Casting: Lizzie Martinez
Cast: Trevor Jack Brooks, Lorelei Linklater, Wiley Wiggins, Glover Gill, Lara
　Hicks, Ames Asbell, Leigh Mahoney, Sara Nelson, Jeanine Attaway, Erik
　Grostic, Bill Wise, Robert C. Solomon, Kim Krizan, Eamonn Healy, J. C.
　Shakespeare, Ethan Hawke, Julie Delpy, Charles Gunning, David Sosa,
　Alex Jones, Otto Hofmann, Aklilu Gebrewold, Carol Dawson, Lisa Moore,
　Steve Fitch, Louis Mackey, Alex Nixon, Violet Nichols, Steven Prince, Ken

Webster, Mary McBay, Kregg A. Foote, Jason T. Hodge, Guy Forsyth, John Christensen, Caveh Zahedi, David Jewell, Adam Goldberg, Nicky Katt, E. Jason Liebrecht, Brent Green, Rc Whittaker, Hymie Samuelson, David Martinez, Ryan Power, Tiana Hux, Speed Levitch, Steve Brudniak, Marta Banda, Steven Soderbergh, Charles Murdock, Mona Lee, Edith Mannix, Bess Cox, Louis Black, Richard Linklater
Color
101 min.

Tape (2001)
USA
Production: The Independent Film Channel Productions, InDigEnt, Detour Filmproduction, Tape Productions
Producers: Anne Walker-McBay, Gary Winick, Alexis Alexanian, Jonathan Sehring, Caroline Kaplan, John Sloss, Robert Cole, David Richenthal
Distribution: Lions Gate Films
Direction: Richard Linklater
Screenplay: Stephen Belber
Cinematography: Maryse Alberti
Editing: Sandra Adair
Production Design: Stephen J. Beatrice
Costume Design: Catherine Thomas
Cast: Ethan Hawke (Vin), Robert Sean Leonard (Jon), Uma Thurman (Amy)
Color
86 min.

Live from Shiva's Dance Floor (2003)
USA
Production: Giraffe Partners, Detour Filmproduction
Producers: Perri Peltz, David Holbrooke, Sarah Holbrooke, Ian Grody
Distribution: Aspyr Media (DVD)
Direction: Richard Linklater
Cinematography: Lee Daniel
Editing: Sandra Adair
Sound: Gerry Stein
Sound Editing and Mixing: Tom Hammond
Original Music: Golden Arm Trio
Tour Guide, Historian, Philosopher, "Cruiser": Timothy "Speed" Levitch
Color
21 min.

The School of Rock (2003)
Germany and USA
Production: Paramount Pictures, Scott Rudin Productions, Detour
   Filmproduction, MFP Munich Film Partners, New Century GmbH & Co.,
   SOR Productions KG
Producers: Scott Rudin, Steve Nicolaides, Scott Aversano
Distribution: Paramount Pictures
Direction: Richard Linklater
Screenplay: Mike White
Cinematography: Rogier Stoffers
Editing: Sandra Adair
Production Design: Jeremy Conway
Costume Design: Karen Patch
Music Score: Craig Wedren
Music Supervisor: Randall Poster
Casting: Ilene Starger
Cast: Jack Black (Dewey Finn), Joan Cusack (Rosalie Mullins), Mike White
   (Ned Schneebly), Sarah Silverman (Patty Di Marco), Lee Wilkof (Mr.
   Green), Kate McGregor-Stewart (Mrs. Lemmons), Adam Pascal (Theo),
   Suzzanne Douglas (Tomika's Mother), Miranda Cosgrove (Summer
   Hathaway), Kevin Clark (Freddy Jones), Joey Gaydos Jr. (Zack), Robert
   Tsai (Lawrence), Aleisha Allen (Alicia), Brian Falduto (Billy), Caitlin
   Hale (Marta), Maryam Hassan (Tomika), Jordan-Claire Green (Michelle),
   Veronica Afflerbach (Eleni), Angelo Massagli (Frankie), Cole Hawkins
   (Leonard), James Hosey (Marco), Zachary Infante (Gordon), Rebecca
   Brown (Katie), Jaclyn Niedenthal (Emily), Tim Hopper (Zack's Father)
Color
109 min.

Before Sunset (2004)
USA
Production: Warner Independent Pictures, Castle Rock Entertainment,
   Detour Filmproduction
Producers: Anne Walker-McBay, John Sloss, Isabelle Coulet
Distribution: Warner Independent Pictures
Direction: Richard Linklater
Screenplay: Richard Linklater, Julie Delpy, Ethan Hawke
Cinematography: Lee Daniel
Editing: Sandra Adair
Production Design: Baptiste Glaymann
Costume Design: Thierry Delettre
Supervising Sound Editing: Tom Hammond
Casting (Paris): Annette Trumel

Cat Handler: Laurent Flaesch
Cast: Ethan Hawke (Jesse), Julie Delpy (Celine), Vernon Dobtcheff
(Bookstore Manager), Louise Lemoine Torres (Journalist #1), Rodolphe
Pauly (Journalist #2), Mariane Plasteig (Waitress), Diabolo (Philippe),
Denis Evrard (Boat Attendant), Albert Delpy (Man at Grill), Marie Pillet
(Woman in Courtyard)
Color
80 min.

Bad News Bears (2005)
USA
Production: Paramount Pictures, Media Talent Group, Detour
Filmproduction
Producers: Marcus Viscidi, J. Geyer Kosinski, Richard Linklater, Bruce
Heller, Brad Marks, Sara Greene, Adam Ellison
Distribution: Paramount Pictures
Direction: Richard Linklater
Screenplay: Bill Lancaster, Glenn Ficarra, John Requa
Cinematography: Rogier Stoffers
Editing: Sandra Adair
Production Design: Bruce Curtis
Costume Design: Karen Patch
Original Music: Edward Shearmur
Music Supervisor: Randall Poster
Casting: Joseph Middleton
Cast: Billy Bob Thornton (Morris Buttermaker), Greg Kinnear (Roy Bullock),
Marcia Gay Harden (Liz Whitewood), Sammi Kane Kraft (Amanda
Whurlitzer), Ridge Canipe (Toby Whitewood), Brandon Craggs (Mike
Engelberg), Jeffrey Davies (Kelly Leak), Timmy Deters (Tanner Boyle),
Carlos Estrada (Miguel Agilar), Emmanuel Estrada (Jose Agilar), Troy
Gentile (Matthew Hooper), Kenneth "K. C." Harris (Ahmad Abdul
Rahim), Aman Johal (Prem Lahiri), Tyler Patrick Jones (Timmy Lupus),
Jeffrey Tedmori (Garo Daragebrigadian), Carter Jenkins (Joey Bullock),
Seth Adkins (Jimmy)
Color
113 min.

A Scanner Darkly (2006)
USA
Production: Warner Independent Pictures, Thousand Words, Section Eight,
Detour Filmproduction, 3 Arts Entertainment
Producers: Erin Ferguson, George Clooney, Steven Soderbergh, Jennifer
Fox, Ben Cosgrove, John Sloss, Palmer West, Jonah Smith, Erwin Stoff,
Anne Walker-McBay, Tommy Pallotta

Distribution: Warner Independent Pictures
Direction: Richard Linklater
Screenplay: Richard Linklater
Head of Animation: Bob Sabiston, Jason Archer, Paul Beck
Cinematography: Shane F. Kelly
Editing: Sandra Adair
Production Design: Bruce Curtis
Costume Design: Kari Perkins
Casting: Denise Chamain
Music: Graham Reynolds
Cast: Keanu Reeves (Bob Arctor), Robert Downey Jr. (James Barris), Woody
    Harrelson (Ernie Luckman), Winona Ryder (Donna Hawthorne), Rory
    Cochrane (Charles Freck), Angela Rawna (Medical Deputy #1), Chamblee
    Ferguson (Medical Deputy #2), Leif Anders (Freck Suicide Narrator),
    Turk Pipkin (Creature), Alex Jones (Street Prophet), Lisa Marie Newmyer
    (Connie), Dameon Clarke (Mike), Marco Perella (Donald)
Color
100 min.

Fast Food Nation (2006)
UK and USA
Production: Fox Searchlight Pictures, Participant Productions, Hanway
    Films, BBC Films, Recorded Picture Company, Detour Filmproduction
Producers: Jeremy Thomas, Malcolm McLaren, Ann Carli, Jeff Skoll, Ricky
    Strauss, Chris Salvaterra, Ed Saxon, Peter Watson, Eric Schlosser, David
    M. Thompson, Alexandra Stone, Sara Greene
Distribution: Fox Searchlight Pictures
Direction: Richard Linklater
Screenplay: Eric Schlosser, Richard Linklater
Cinematography: Lee Daniel
Editing: Sandra Adair
Production Design: Bruce Curtis
Costume Design: Kari Perkins, Lee Hunsaker
Music: Friends of Dean Martinez
Cast: Patricia Arquette (Cindy), Bobby Cannavale (Mike), Paul Dano (Brian),
    Luis Guzman (Benny), Ethan Hawke (Pete), Ashley Johnson (Amber),
    Greg Kinnear (Don Anderson), Kris Kristofferson (Rudy Martin),
    Avril Lavigne (Alice), Esai Morales (Tony), Catalina Sandino Moreno
    (Sylvia), Lou Taylor Pucci (Paco), Ana Claudia Talancón (Coco), Wilmer
    Valderrama (Raul), Bruce Willis (Harry Rydell)
Color
113 min.

Inning by Inning: A Portrait of a Coach (2008)
USA
Production: Detour Filmproduction
Producers: Brian Franklin, Connor Schell, John Sloss, Sandra Adair, Sara
    Greene, Daniel Silver
Distribution: ESPN Films
Direction: Richard Linklater
Cinematography: Brian Franklin, Anton Poimtsev, Kevin Ford
Editing: Sandra Adair
Original Score: Michael McLeod
Color
106 min.

Me and Orson Welles (2009)
UK and USA
Production: CinemaNX, Isle of Man Film, Framestore Features, Hart/
    Lunsford Pictures, Detour Filmproduction
Producers: Richard Linklater, Marc Samuelson, Ann Carli, Steve Christian,
    John Sloss, Steve Norris, Holly Gent Palmo, Vince Palmo, Andrew Fingret,
    Jessica Parker, Sara Greene, Richard Hewitt
Distribution: Hart/Lunsford Pictures, CinemaNX, Cinetic Media, Pandemic
    Marketing, Freestyle Releasing
Direction: Richard Linklater
Screenplay: Holly Gent Palmo, Vince Palmo
Cinematography: Dick Pope
Editing: Sandra Adair
Production Design: Laurence Dorman
Hair and Make-Up Design: Fae Hammond
Costume Design: Nic Ede
Music Supervisor: Marc Marot
Casting: Lucy Bevan
Cast: Ben Chaplin (George Coulouris), Claire Danes (Sonja Jones), Zac
    Efron (Richard Samuels), Zoe Kazan (Gretta Adler), Eddie Marsan
    (John Houseman), Christian McKay (Orson Welles), Kelly Reilly (Muriel
    Brassler), James Tupper (Joseph Cotton), Leo Bill (Norman Lloyd), Patrick
    Kennedy (Grover Burgess), Aidan McArdle (Martin Gabel), Al Weaver
    (Sam Leve), Thomas Arnold (George Duthie), Megan Maczko (Evelyn
    Allen), Jo McInnes (Jeannie Rosenthal), Iain McKee (Vakhtangov), Simon
    Nehan (Joe Holland), Travis Oliver (John Hoyt), Simon Lee Phillips
    (Walter Ash), Daniel Tuite (William Mowry)
Color
114 min.

Andrew, Dudley. *What Cinema Is! Bazin's "Quest" and Its Charge.* Chichester, England: Wiley-Blackwell, 2010. Print.

Astruc, Alexandre. "The Birth of a New Avant-Garde: *La caméra-stylo.*" *The New Wave.* Ed. Peter Graham. Garden City, NY: Doubleday, 1968. 16–23. Print.

Barthes, Roland. *The Grain of the Voice: Interviews, 1962–1980.* Trans. Linda Coverdale. 1985. Berkeley and Los Angeles: U of California P, 1991. Print.

Baumgarten, Marjorie. "Black and White and Rick All Over: The ABCs of *The School of Rock.*" *Austin Chronicle.* Austin Chronicle, 3 Oct. 2003: n. pag. Web. 8 Sept. 2010.

Bazin, André. *What Is Cinema?* Vol. 1. Ed. and trans. Hugh Gray. Berkeley and Los Angeles: U of California P, 1967. Print.

"*Before Sunset* Production Notes." Warner Independent. Wip.warnerbros.com: n. pag. Web. 6 Apr 2009.

Belber, Stephen. *Tape.* In *Humana Festival 2000: The Complete Plays.* Ed. Michael Bigelow Dixon and Amy Wegener. Hanover: Smith and Kraus, 2000. 1–45. Print.

Bellafante, Ginia. "Finding Room for an Actor Fit for the Stage." *New York Times.* New York Times, 6 June 2007: n. pag. Web. 12 Jan. 2010.

Beuka, Robert. *SuburbiaNation: Reading Suburban Landscape in Twentieth-Century American Fiction and Film.* New York: Palgrave Macmillan, 2004. Print.

Black, Louis. "On His Mark." *Austin Chronicle.* Austin Chronicle, 11 Dec. 2009: n. pag. Web. 23 Apr. 2010.

———. "Page Two: Reform School." *Austin Chronicle.* Austin Chronicle, 22 Jan. 2010: n. pag. Web. 27 Oct. 2010.

———. "Take Two." *Texas Monthly.* Texas Monthly, Oct. 1992: n. pag. Web. 8 Mar. 2010.

Bogosian, Eric. *subUrbia* (play). New York: Theatre Communications Group, 1995. Print.

———. *subUrbia* (screenplay). New York: St. Martin's, 1997. Print.

Bonomo, Joe. *Highway to Hell.* New York: Continuum, 2010. Print.

———. "Re: Question on AC/DC from a Film Scholar." Message to the author. 15 Sept. 2010. Email.

Bordwell, David. *The Way Hollywood Tells It: Story and Style in Modern Movies.* Berkeley and Los Angeles: U of California P, 2006. Print.

Caldwell, John T. "Welcome to the Viral Future of Cinema (Television)." *Cinema Journal* 45.1 (2005): 90–97. *JSTOR.* Web. 23 Nov. 2010.

Callow, Simon. *Orson Welles: The Road to Xanadu.* New York: Viking, 1995. Print.

Carrère, Emmanuel. *I Am Alive and You Are Dead: A Journey into the Mind of Philip K. Dick.* Trans. Timothy Bent. 1993. New York: Picador, 2004. Print.

Christie, Thomas A. *The Cinema of Richard Linklater.* 2nd ed. Maidstone, England: Crescent Moon, 2011. Print.

Ciampa, Su. "Ground Zero: Where the Buffalo Roam?" *Salon.com.* Salon Media Group, 21 Jan. 2003. Web. 9 Jan 2011.

Conrad, Peter. *Orson Welles: The Stories of His Life.* London: Faber and Faber, 2003. Print.

Corrigan, Timothy. *A Cinema without Walls: Movies and Culture after Vietnam.* New Brunswick: Rutgers UP, 1991. Print.

Coward, Noël. *Still Life.* In *Plays: Three.* London: Eyre Methuen, 1979. 335–81. Print.

The Cruise. Dir. Bennett Miller. Artisan Entertainment, 1998. Streaming web video.

Dargis, Manohla. "The Kids Are Alright; The Coach Has Problems." *New York Times* 22 July 2005: E13. *LexisNexis Academic.* Web. 12 Oct. 2010.

Dawtrey, Adam. "CinemaNX Boards Trio." *Variety.* Variety, 18 May 2008: n. pag. Web. 22 Dec. 2010.

———. "European Film Sales Struggling." *Variety.* Variety, 28 Aug. 2008: n. pag. Web. 22 Dec. 2010.

"A Decade in the Dark: 2000–2009." *Film Comment* Jan.–Feb. 2010: 26–43. *Academic Search Premier.* Web. 13 Jan. 2010.

DeFore, John. "Richard Linklater's *Inning by Inning* Follows Coach Augie Garrido." *American-Statesman.* Austin360.com, 2 June 2008: n. pag. Web. 29 Nov. 2010.

Dick, Philip K. *A Scanner Darkly.* 1977. New York: Vintage, 1991. Print.

"*Fast Food Nation* Press Kit." *Festival-cannes.com.* Festival de Cannes Archives. Web. 8 Nov. 2010.

Flanagan, Hallie. *Arena: The History of the Federal Theatre.* 1940. New York: Benjamin Bloom, 1965. Print.

Geuens, Jean-Pierre. "The Digital World Picture." *Film Quarterly* 55.4 (2002): 16–27. *JSTOR.* Web. 29 Aug. 2008.

Ginsberg, Allen. *Howl, and Other Poems.* 1956. San Francisco: City Lights, 1993. Print.

Goodman, Paul. *Growing Up Absurd: Problems of Youth in the Organized Society.* New York: Vintage, 1960. Print.

Griffin, John. "Be Seduced by a Sunny Afternoon in Paris: Follow-up to 1995's *Before Sunrise;* Two Great Actors and a Great Director Make Us Believe in the Possibility of True Love." *Gazette* [Montreal] 9 July 2004: D1. *LexisNexis Academic.* Web. 27 Sept. 2010.

Gunning, Tom. "Moving Away from the Index: Cinema and the Impression of Reality." *Differences: A Journal of Feminist Cultural Studies* 18.1 (2007): 29–52. Print.

Hadjioannou, Markos. "*Waking Life:* The Destiny of Cinema's Dreamscape; or, The Question of Old *and* New Mediations." *Excursions* 1.1 (2010): 53–72. *Excursions-journal.org.uk.* Web. 3 Aug. 2010.

Harrod, Mary. "The Aesthetics of Pastiche in the Work of Richard Linklater." *Screen* 51.1 (2010): 21–37. Print.

Hernandez, Raoul. "Bigger Stakes: Richard Linklater on Remixing *The Bad News Bears.*" *Austin Chronicle.* Austin Chronicle, 29 July 2005: n. pag. Web. 12 Oct. 2010.

Hill, Derek. *Charlie Kaufman and Hollywood's Merry Band of Pranksters, Fabulists, and Dreamers: An Excursion into the American New Wave.* Harpenden, England: Kamera Books, 2008. Print.

Holden, Stephen. "Cacophony in Three Parts." *New York Times* 2 Nov. 2001: E1. *LexisNexis Academic.* Web. 9 Aug. 2010.

Houpt, Simon. "This, after *Before Sunset?*" *Globe and Mail* [Toronto] 21 July 2005: R3. *LexisNexis Academic.* Web. 12 Oct. 2010.

Isaacs, Edith J. R. "When Good Men Get Together: Broadway in Review." *Theatre Arts Monthly* 22.1 (1938): 11–22. Print.

Italie, Hillel. "What Price the Off-Hollywood Shuffle?" *Associated Press* 25 Aug. 1991: BC Cycle. *LexisNexis Academic.* Web. 28 Jan. 2010.

Jameson, Fredric. *Postmodernism, or, The Cultural Logic of Late Capitalism.* Durham: Duke UP, 1991. Print.

———. "Postmodernism and Consumer Society." *The Anti-Aesthetic: Essays on Postmodern Culture.* Ed. Hal Foster. New York: New Press, 1998. 127–44. Print.

Johnson, David T. "Directors on Adaptation: A Conversation with Richard Linklater." *Literature/Film Quarterly* 35.1 (2007): 338–41. Print.

Kaplow, Robert. *Me and Orson Welles.* New York: Penguin, 2003. Print.

Kay, Jeremy. "Cinemanx Finalises US Distribution for *Me And Orson Welles.*" *Screendaily.* Screen International, 9 Sept. 2009. Web. 31 May 2011.

Keats, John. "To Benjamin Bailey, November 22, 1817 [Hampstead]." *English Romantic Writers.* Ed. David Perkins. San Diego: Harcourt Brace Jovanovich, 1967. Print.

Klinger, Barbara. *Beyond the Multiplex: Cinema, New Technologies, and the Home.* Berkeley and Los Angeles: U of California P, 2006. Print.

Koresky, Michael, and Jeff Reichert. "A Conversation with Richard Linklater." *Reverse Shot Online*. Reverse Shot Online, Summer 2004. Web. 28 Jan 2010.

La Franco, Robert. "Trouble in Toontown." *Wired*. Wired, March 2006: n. pag. Web. 28 Oct. 2010.

Leitch, Thomas. "Twice-Told Tales: Disavowal and the Rhetoric of the Remake." *Dead Ringers: The Remake in Theory and Practice*. Ed. Jennifer Forrest and Leonard R. Koos. Albany: SUNY Press, 2002. 37–62. Print.

Linklater, Richard. "Commentary—*It's Impossible to Learn to Plow by Reading Books*." *Slacker*. Criterion, 2004. DVD. Disc 2.

———. "Director's Statement" (inset essay). *Live from Shiva's Dance Floor*. Aspyr, 2003. DVD.

———. *Slacker*. New York: St. Martin's, 1992. Print.

Linklater, Richard, and Ethan Hawke. "Commentary with Richard Linklater & Ethan Hawke." *Tape*. Lion's Gate Home Entertainment, 2001. DVD.

Linklater, Richard, Denise Montgomery, and friends. *Dazed and Confused*. New York: St. Martin's, 1993. Print.

Linklater, Richard, et al. *Before Sunrise and Before Sunset*. New York: Vintage, 2005. Print.

Linklater, Richard, et al. "Commentary by the Filmmakers." *Waking Life*. Twentieth Century Fox Home Entertainment, 2002. DVD.

Macaulay, Scott. "The Schizoid Man." *Filmmaker*. Filmmaker, Winter 2006: n. pag. Web. 28 Oct. 2010.

Macor, Alison. *Chainsaws, Slackers, and Spy Kids: Thirty Years of Filmmaking in Austin, Texas*. Austin: U of Texas P, 2010. Print.

Marshall, Lee. "Love That Goes with the Flow[.] Nine Years after Their First Film, Ethan Hawke and Julie Delpy Are Reunited for an Unusual Sequel. They Tell Lee Marshall about the Overlap between Life and Art." *Sunday Telegraph* [London] 18 July 2004: 7. *LexisNexis Academic*. Web. 27 Sept. 2010.

McGann, Jerome. *Radiant Textuality: Literature after the World Wide Web*. New York: Palgrave, 2001. Print.

Monaco, James. *The New Wave: Truffaut, Godard, Chabrol, Rohmer, Rivette*. New York: Oxford UP, 1976. Print.

Murphy, J. J. *Me and You and Memento and Fargo: How Independent Screenplays Work*. New York: Continuum, 2007. Print.

Naremore, James. "Films of the Year, 2009." *Film Quarterly* 63.4 (2010): 18–32. Print.

———. *The Magic World of Orson Welles*. 1978. Dallas: Southern Methodist UP, 1989. Print.

Neale, Steve. *Genre and Hollywood*. London: Routledge, 2000. Print.

Newton, Willis, and Joe Newton (as told to Claude Stanush and David Middleton). *The Newton Boys: Portrait of an Outlaw Gang*. Austin: State House, 1994. Print.

Ng, Jenna. "Virtual Cinematography and the Digital Real: (Dis)placing the Moving Image between Reality and Simulacra." *The State of the Real: Aesthetics in the Digital Age.* Ed. Damian Sutton, Susan Brind, and Ray McKenzie. London: I. B. Tauris, 2007. Print.

Norton, Glen. "The Seductive Slack of *Before Sunrise.*" *Post Script* 19.2 (2000): 62–72. Print.

Palmer, Christopher. *Philip K. Dick: Exhilaration and Terror of the Postmodern.* Liverpool: Liverpool UP, 2003. Print.

Peary, Gerald. "*Bad News Bears:* Parables in a Ball Park." *Jump Cut* 14 (1977): 35. Ejumpcut.org. Web. 7 Oct. 2010.

Pevere, Geoff. "Minds That Make Out." *Toronto Star* 9 July 2004: C1. *LexisNexis Academic.* Web. 27 Sept. 2010.

Pichler, Barbara. "An Iconography of the Midwest." *James Benning.* Ed. Barbara Pichler and Claudia Slanar. Vienna: Synema Publikationen, 2007. 21–46. Print.

Pierson, John. *Spike, Mike, Slackers & Dykes.* New York: Hyperion, 1995. Print.

Polan, Dana. "*Bad News Bears:* Sour American Dream." *Jump Cut* 15 (1977): 9–10. Ejumpcut.org. Web. 7 Oct. 2010.

Pope, S. W. *Patriotic Games: Sporting Traditions in the American Imagination, 1876–1926.* 1997. Knoxville: U of Tennessee P, 2007. Print.

Price, Brian. "Richard Linklater." *Senses of Cinema* 25 July 2003. Web. 31 Dec 2010.

Radwan, Jon. "Generation X and Postmodern Cinema: *Slacker.*" *Post Script* 19.2 (2000): 34–48. Print.

Ray, Robert B. *The Avant-Garde Finds Andy Hardy.* Cambridge: Harvard UP, 1995. Print.

Rea, Steven. "Romantics Win: *Sunset* Follows *Sunrise.*" *Philadelphia Inquirer* 4 July 2004: H7. *LexisNexis Academic.* Web. 27 Sept. 2010.

Reichert, Jeff. "Rock 'n' Roll Middle School." *Reverse Shot Online.* Reverse Shot Online, Summer 2004. Web. 16 Sept. 2010.

Restuccio, Daniel. "InDigEnt's Cost-effective, Digital Philosophy." *Post.* Postmagazine.com. 1 Oct. 2003. Web. 9 Jan. 2011.

Robey, Tim. "The Best Years in the Life of Richard Linklater." *Sight & Sound* Apr. 2007: 24–27. Print.

Robson, Tom. "Field of American Dreams: Individualist Ideology in the U.S. Baseball Movie." *Jump Cut* 52 (Summer 2010). Ejumpcut.org. Web. 7 Oct. 2010.

Rodowick, D. N. *The Virtual Life of Film.* Cambridge: Harvard UP, 2007. Print.

Rosa, Jorge Martins. "A Misreading Gone Too Far? Baudrillard Meets Philip K. Dick." *Science Fiction Studies* 35 (2008): 60–71. *Academic Search Premier.* Web. 25 Oct. 2010.

Rosenbaum, Jonathan. "Open Spaces." *Chicago Reader* 3 Apr. 1998. Jonathan-rosenbaum.com. Web. 14 June 2010.

Rowin, Michael Joshua. "Mortal Beloved." *Reverse Shot Online.* Reverse Shot Online, Summer 2004. Web. 5 Oct. 2010.

Schlosser, Eric. *Fast Food Nation: The Dark Side of the All-American Meal.* 2001. New York: Harper Perennial, 2005. Print.

"*The School of Rock* Handbook of Production Information." Hollywood: Paramount Pictures Publicity Department, 2003. Print.

Sellier, Geneviève. *Masculine Singular: French New Wave Cinema.* Trans. Kristin Ross. Durham: Duke UP, 2008. Print.

Shaviro, Steven. "Emotion Capture: Affect in Digital Film." *Projections* 1:2 (2007): 37–56. Print.

Shumway, David R. "Rock 'n' Roll Sound Tracks and the Production of Nostalgia." *Cinema Journal* 38.2 (1999): 36–51. *JSTOR.* Web. 1 Feb. 2010.

Sitney, P. Adams. *Visionary Film: The American Avant-Garde.* New York: Oxford UP, 1974. Print.

Slouka, Mark. "Dehumanized: When Math and Science Rule the School." *Harper's* Sept. 2009: 32–40. Print.

Smith, Damon. "A Love Story to Send You into Swoons of Giddy Delight." *Bath Chronicle* 23 July 2004: Features 2. *LexisNexis Academic.* Web. 27 Sept. 2010.

Speed, Lesley. "The Possibilities of Roads Not Taken: Intellect and Utopia in the Films of Richard Linklater." *Journal of Popular Film & Television* 35.3 (2007): 98–106. *Academic Search Premier.* Web. 1 Nov. 2010.

———. "Tuesday's Gone." *Journal of Popular Film & Television* 26.1 (1998): 24–32. *Communication & Mass Media Complete.* Web. 4 Apr. 2011.

Spong, John. "The Spirit of '76." *Texas Monthly.* Texas Monthly, Oct. 2003: n. pag. Web. 4 Mar. 2010.

Stanush, Claude. "Barbed Wire." *Smithsonian* Sept. 1991: 13. *Academic Search Premier.* Web. 13 June 2010.

———. "'Every Time a Bank Was Robbed, They Thought It Was Us.'" *Smithsonian* Jan. 1994: 74–82. *Academic Search Premier.* Web. 13 June 2010.

Stone, D. Z. "A Teacher's Dream Gets to the Screen." *New York Times.* New York Times, 13 Nov. 2009: NJ12. Web. 20 Dec. 2010.

Sutin, Lawrence. *Divine Invasions: A Life of Philip K. Dick.* New York: Harmony, 1989. Print.

Syngle, Erik. "Love Me Tonight." *Reverse Shot Online.* Reverse Shot Online, Summer 2004. Web. 7 Apr. 2010.

Teaford, Jon C. *The American Suburb: The Basics.* New York: Routledge, 2008. Print.

Thoreau, Henry David. *Walden and Civil Disobedience.* 1854, 1849. Ed. Sherman Paul. Boston: Houghton Mifflin, 1960. Print.

Turner, Lynn. "Wind Up: The Machine-Event of *Tape.*" *Camera Obscura* 64 (2007): 112–35. *Academic Search Premier.* Web. 5 Aug. 2010.

Ulmer, Gregory L. [posting as "glue"]. "Bureaucracy of the Imagination." *Routine: The Coming Internet Theory:* n. pag. 13 Aug. 2010. Web. 9 Jan. 2011.

Varda, Agnès. *Remembrances* (2005). *4 by Agnès Varda.* Criterion, 2007. DVD.

Vaughan, Dai. *For Documentary: Twelve Essays.* Berkeley and Los Angeles: U of California P, 1999. Print.

Warnet, J. R. "An Interview with Robert Kaplow, Author of *Me and Orson Welles.*" *Alternative Press.* Alternative Press, 21 Dec. 2009: n. pag. Web. 12 Jan. 2011.

Webb, Walter Prescott. *The Great Plains.* Boston: Ginn, 1931. Print.

Weeks, Jerome. "Texas Artists Place Ad Against Bush[.] It Will Run in Key States; Group Doesn't Attack Specific Policies." *Dallas Morning News* 18 Oct. 2004: A7. *LexisNexis Academic.* Web. 27 Sept. 2010.

Williams, Linda. "Mirrors without Memories: Truth, History, and *The Thin Blue Line.*" *Documenting the Documentary: Close Readings of Documentary Film and Video.* Ed. Barry Keith Grant and Jeannette Sloniowski. Detroit: Wayne State UP, 1998. 379–96. Print.

Wolfe, Thomas. *Look Homeward, Angel.* New York: Scribner's, 1929. Print.

Wood, Robin. *Sexual Politics and Narrative Film: Hollywood and Beyond.* New York: Columbia UP, 1998. Print.

Worland, Rick, and Edward Countryman. "The New Western American Historiography and the Emergence of the New American Westerns." *Back in the Saddle Again: New Essays on the Western.* Ed. Edward Buscombe and Roberta E. Pearson. London: BFI, 1998. 182–96. Print.

Index |

Kinski, Klaus, 7, 38
Klinger, Barbara, 112
Koresky, Michael, 20, 37, 88
Kraft, Sammi Kane, 89
Krizan, Kim, 132
Kubelka, Peter, 14

La Collectionneuse (1967), 29
Lancaster, Bill, 90
Lanzmann, Claude, 63
La Passion de Jeanne d'Arc (1928), 16
L'argent (1983), 6
League of Their Own, A (1992), 112
Lean, David, 35
Led Zeppelin, 76
Leigh, Janet, 145
Leitch, Thomas, 91
Leonard, Robert Sean, 61
Leve, Samuel (Sam), 121, 123
Levitch, Timothy "Speed": in *Live from Shiva's Dance Floor*, 9, 54, 68–74, 139; and "portrait" film, 114, 146; in *Waking Life*, 59
Linklater, Richard: allusions in cinema of, 5–7; and *Bad News Bears*, 89–95, 142; and *Before Sunrise*, 33–40, 132–33; and *Before Sunset*, 81–89, 140–41; and collaboration, 3, 19, 130–32, 140–41, 147; criticism about, 4–5; and *Dazed and Confused*, 26–33, 131–32; and defiance of authorial pattern, 1–3, 95; early life of, 12, 128–30; and *Fast Food Nation*, 103–10, 143–45; and *$5.15/ Hr.*, 104, 142; and genre, 13–14, 28–29, 48–49, 95, 110; and independent cinema, 19–20, 147; and *Inning by Inning: A Portrait of a Coach*, 110–17, 145–46; interview with, 127–49; and *It's Impossible to Learn to Plow by Reading Books*, 12–18, 129–30; and *Live from Shiva's Dance Floor*, 68–74, 138–39; and *Me and Orson Welles*, 117–24, 146–47; motifs in cinema of, 15, 32, 43, 71–72, 97; and *The Newton Boys*, 47–54, 135–36; and nostalgia, 27–28; and politics, 93–94, 104–5, 143–44; and remakes, 90–92; and Romanticism, 3, 110, 124; and *A Scan-*

ner Darkly, 96–103, 142–43; and *The School of Rock*, 74–81, 139–40; and *Slacker*, 18–26, 130–31; and *subUrbia*, 40–47, 133–34; and *Tape*, 61–68, 137–38; and Thoreau, 7–11, 44, 59, 72, 73; and *Waking Life*, 54–61, 136–37. *See also* cinematography; creativity; editing; narrative; passion; time
Live from Shiva's Dance Floor (2003): and America, 71–74; analysis of, 68–74; and attendance to the present, 9; and "cruising," 69–70; and Ground Zero, 68–74; and imagination, 72–73; and *Inning by Inning*, 72; and Linklater's politics, 104; and memorial, 68–74; and New York City, 70–71; principal cast and crew of, 156; production history of, 68, 138–39; and *A Scanner Darkly*, 72; and *The School of Rock*, 72; and *subUrbia*, 72; and *Waking Life*, 139; and Wall Street, 69–70
Look Homeward, Angel, 83
Lucas, George, 6

Mackey, Louis, 7
Macor, Alison, 3–4, 47
Mad Men (2007–), 41
Malle, Louis, 54
Marcus, Scott, 23
Marey, Étienne-Jules, 66
Matrix, The (1999), 98
Matthau, Walter, 89
McCarty, Kathy, 23, 34
McConaughey, Matthew, 135
McCormack, Keith, 13
McDonald's (corporation), 106
McGann, Jerome, 125
McKay, Christian, 117, 120
McLaren, Malcolm, 103
Me and Orson Welles (novel), 117, 118, 121, 123
Me and Orson Welles (2009) (film): and allusions, 7; analysis of, 117–24; and attendance to the present, 10, 123–24; criticism of, 121–22; and images of Welles, 120–22; and *It's Impossible to Learn to Plow by Reading Books*, 123; and Kaplow's novel, 117, 118, 121, 123;

David T. Johnson is an associate professor
of English at Salisbury University and the coeditor of
*Conversations with Directors: An Anthology of Interviews
from* Literature/Film Quarterly.

Books in the series
Contemporary Film Directors

Jacques Rivette
  Mary M. Wiles

Kim Ki-duk
  Hye Seung Chung

Philip Kaufman
  Annette Insdorf

Richard Linklater
  David T. Johnson

The University of Illinois Press
is a founding member of the
Association of American University Presses.

Designed by Paula Newcomb
Composed in 10/13 New Caledonia LT Std
with Helvetica Neue LT Std display
by Barbara Evans
at the University of Illinois Press
Manufactured by Sheridan Books, Inc.

University of Illinois Press
1325 South Oak Street
Champaign, IL 61820-6903
www.press.uillinois.edu